INDUSTRIAL DISCIPLINE
and the
ARBITRATION PROCESS

•

ROBERT H. SKILTON

•

Published for the
LABOR RELATIONS COUNCIL
of the
WHARTON SCHOOL OF FINANCE AND COMMERCE
by the
UNIVERSITY OF PENNSYLVANIA PRESS
Philadelphia
1952

Robert H. Skilton is a member of the Philadelphia Bar and Associate Professor of Business Law at the Wharton School, University of Pennsylvania. He served as a wage analyst for the War Department in 1943. He is the author of *Government and the Mortgage Debtor, 1929-1939,* and of articles in various publications. He has served as arbitrator in labor disputes.

CONTENTS

ACKNOWLEDGMENT

The writer acknowledges the generous advice and counsel of Dr. George W. Taylor in the preparation of this paper.

PREFACE

As unions and management develop their collective-bargaining relationships, they encounter a long series of separate and distinctive industrial relations problems which must be individually grappled with and finally resolved. For example, wage-rate and seniority problems are two among many which have their own peculiarities. One of the most important of these problems relates to management discipline of employees under the collective-bargaining agreement and under arbitration. It is this matter of discipline which is brought into sharp focus by Robert H. Skilton in his monograph entitled *Industrial Discipline and the Arbitration Process.* He bases his study principally upon an analysis of published awards of arbitrators and, in so doing, makes a very significant contribution to the available writings on this subject,

There can be little doubt that the advent of collective bargaining usually brings about the necessity for a reëvaluation by management of how its discipline function will be carried out. Here is a function, heretofore unilaterally exercised, which becomes subject to joint determination. It is significant that, under most collective agreements, management has retained the right to initiate disciplinary action but has had to assume the obligation of justifying that action as being for just cause. When the union is unconvinced on the point, it is customary under most labor agreements to submit the question to arbitration.

Basically then, collective bargaining has come to mean that the union has not sought directly to participate in the formulation of a discipline policy. Its participation is indirect as expressed in challenges to certain disciplinary actions either in the grievance procedure or before the arbitrator. Great advantages for management and the union derive from such an approach as compared, for instance, with the use of work stoppages in protest against disciplinary actions or with direct negotiations for an all-inclusive discipline policy. At the same time, great responsibilities are assigned to the arbitrator who is called upon to decide whether or not a certain discipline was actually for just cause. The security or the job of an individual employee is at stake. Involved also is the degree of job security to be enjoyed by the workers as a group, for, like it or not, precedents are established by arbitrators' awards. At the same time, management is properly concerned with preserving its authority to invoke such discipline as is essential for the proper operation of the business. Management also must maintain the employee's will to coöperate, which requires avoidance of disciplinary action considered by the workers to be arbitrary or unjust.

No simple task is given to the arbitrator who is assigned the duty of determining whether or not a disciplinary action taken by management was for just cause. How arbitrators have met that responsibility is the subject—of great industrial-relations importance—dealt with by Robert Skilton. Out of his analysis comes an appreciation of the perplexities faced by these arbitrators. More important, the study is replete with ideas about how unions and managements can assist their arbitrators in performing their duties more effectively. *Industrial Discipline and the Arbitration Process* will doubtless be a valuable aid to unions and managements which seek to improve the results of their collective-bargaining relationship as respects disciplinary actions.

GEORGE W. TAYLOR

Philadelphia
July 1952

INDUSTRIAL DISCIPLINE AND THE ARBITRATION PROCESS

This society of ours, which may still be classed as a society by agreement rather than fiat, has devised contracts of infinite variety. Three contract types which especially have helped to characterize the twentieth century are insurance contracts, credit contracts, and labor contracts.

These contract types, dealing with fields so different and extensive, were developed to meet important human needs. By the self-help of agreement, people have found a way of distributing risk and of minimizing the incidence of economic and legal loss (insurance), of facilitating the distribution of goods and services without cash on the barrelhead (credit contracts), and achieving a measure of industrial peace and co-prosperity (collective-bargaining agreements).

The first two contract types usually involve a group (corporation) and an individual. The third involves a group (the employer) and another group (the union). Thus in all cases the combination of people into a group, be it an insurance company, a bank, or a labor union, has been found desirable to surmount the inadequacy of individual economic power to meet the need to be served.

Unlike the insurance and the credit contract, however, the collective-bargaining agreement is not the end of the negotiation. It does not attempt to treat and delineate all the situations that may confront the parties. The labor agreement is just one significant event in the continuous collective bargaining that goes on between management and union. Much is left to be decided by future negotiation or, if that fails, by arbitration. The labor agreement is, of course, a "legal" contract specifying the conditions under which individual contracts of employment will be made, but much of its interpretation, implementation, and enforcement is beyond the province of the courts.

Consider, for example, the bearing of the labor agreement upon one of the employer's most necessary prerogatives, his power to discipline employees. The importance of this function of management, in terms of production, efficiency, job security, indeed, in terms of all of the relations between the parties, is obvious. The intertwined fate of company and workers depends on the maintenance of discipline. The entire collective-bargaining process depends on proper discipline. Of such things the contract between the parties should speak, but so important is the matter, so variable the situations which may challenge the employer's disciplinary prerogative, that typically the contract will leave much unsaid, to be settled as the occasion arises by day-to-day bargaining between the parties, and by the judgment of an arbitrator.

The Employer's Common Law Prerogative of Discharge and Discipline

Every employer will tell you that when it comes to dealing with his employees, times are not what they used to be. Whether he deems them better, or worse, or as imperfect as usual, will depend upon personal attitude and personal experience. For if there is one thing that is true about disciplinary problems, it is the difficulty of drawing generalizations.

Admittedly, the employer's power to discipline workers has been restricted by collective bargaining. The employer's prerogative until a few years ago was the prerogative of the big stick. The chains of the apprentice system had been broken in the industrial era; bondage and corporal punishment were no more. Still the employer had extensive powers over the job tenure of employees. He did not have to stand for much from his men. With virtual legal impunity, he could fine, demote, transfer, suspend, and fire, according to his pleasure, subject only to the higher laws of practicality and conscience.

There was little in the law of contracts to deter him. Agreements of employment were usually oral and did not specify any definite term. The men were simply hired at so much per day or week or month. Under these circumstances, the employer could discharge without notice at any time, without liability except possibly for the balance of pay for the period mentioned in the rate. The question of the cause for discharge did not come up. Even though the employee had understood that he was being hired on a permanent basis, he would get short shrift in the courts if he had not tied the employer down to a certain minimum term. The judge would talk about the necessity of agreements having to be "definite" to be enforceable.

To be sure, if the employer was to justify a discharge under contracts for a term, he would have to prove that the employee had furnished him grounds for dismissal. But "power" and "right" were two different things. The employer still had the power to dismiss any employee, even though he had no cause and therefore no right. No one, said the common law, could be forced to continue to employ another, to tolerate his presence and his agency. Reinstatement? Unheard of! So suppose the employer did discharge the man, in spite of the contract? The aggrieved had the unhappy prospect of doing battle in legal tournament against the stout champions of his employer, and winding up, even if successful, with money damages which were hardly compensation because he would have to share them with his attorney. It is no wonder that the number of suits for breach of contract of employment to reach appellate courts is rather small.

That employers were for the most part free to do as they pleased in precollective-bargaining days did not mean that in fact they acted with capricious license. Most employers were too sensible to be arbitrary. Doubtless when a worker was discharged or otherwise disciplined, the employer generally felt that he had good and sufficient reason. There were the restraints of morality and common decency. And if some had no morality, at least they knew that labor, like goods, should not be wasted. Whatever restraints they exercised, however, were largely self-imposed.

Common Law Decisions on Just Cause for Discharge

"Just cause" for discharge was involved as a defense in the relatively few instances when the employer was sued for breach of a term contract of employment. In cases of this sort, common law courts did some ground-breaking. Long before arbitrators talked of these things, the courts recognized and identified the now familiar passwords of discharge for cause: incompetence, insubordination, disloyalty, fighting, etc., and drew distinctions between the material and the immaterial.

The language of judges and the language of arbitrators sometimes sound much the same. This should be expected. Many arbitrators are lawyers, many have the advantage of arguments of counsel for the parties. Sometimes arbitrators cite law cases in their opinions.

But does this mean that arbitration is simply the child (without benefit of clergy) of the common law? Definitely not. Rather they are cousins of common stock. The common stock in their veins is the general concept of justice, fairness, ethics, good industrial relations, which are scarcely the exclusive property of judges or arbitrators.

Then there are the differences as well as the similarities. Judges operate in the atmosphere of law. They talk about contract and breach of contract. They defer to the rule of precedent. In a discharge case, the employer is either right or wrong—he cannot be half right and half wrong. Either he is liable for damages or he is not. Hence judges cannot afford to wander through the shady field of mitigating circumstances as arbitrators do. For an arbitrator's award can cut the grievance in half; for example, an arbitrator can reinstate but deny back pay.

The Salient Difference—No Common Law of Arbitration

Judges respect the rule of precedent. Some have carried the principle of consistency to the point where they believe that they should not only be consistent with themselves but also with their ancestors. Their opinions are largely given over to the dusty, pedestrian job of comparing and distinguishing previously decided cases which in turn compared and distinguished other cases and so on ad infinitum. Of course their real thinking processes may differ from the explanations they record for posterity. But there is no doubt that citations are the arms of a lawyer and the crutch of a judge. Even when a judge decides to depart from precedent, he will generally bow deferentially as he backs away.

Arbitrators, on the other hand, frequently operate in the pioneer environment of no precedent. It is every man for himself. Arbitrators do not disrespect the opinions of others. Arbitration is simply not a legal *system*—there is no integration, there is no lower court with an appellate court to reverse it. Nor is there continuity of the arbitration office. There is not the learned secretariat upon which the rule of precedent depends. One arbitrator has declared:

> The Company has submitted a brief in support of its position in which it cites several decisions by other arbitrators, as well as decisions under the National Labor Relations Act, in support of the proposition that the countermanding of management's instructions by a union official, or the use of abusive language by an employee, constitutes grounds for disciplinary action. Such decisions, while interesting, are not binding upon the Arbitrator. The principle of *stare decisis* does not apply in labor arbitration and, in the opinion of the Arbitrator, justifiably so. Were it otherwise, much of the value of present day labor arbitration, reflecting day to day determinations of conflicting equities based upon the peculiar facts of each case, would eventually be lost. It is to be noted that the courts, when confronted with labor cases, have generally limited themselves to the enforcement or interpretation of constitutional, statutory, or contractual rights, and otherwise leave parties to resolve their disputes within the economic arena. Labor and management both look with disfavor upon the utilization of prior decisions by other arbitrators as binding precedents, although this point of view has not prevented either side, in the experience of this Arbitrator, from citing to the arbitrator cases previously decided in their favor on similar issues by other arbitrators. The use of prior decisions as binding precedents was recently criticized in an editorial which appeared in the *New York World-Telegram* on January 30, 1948.

Particularly in cases arising out of the discharge of employees would the use of prior cases as binding precedents be unfortunate. A decision in such a case requires an appraisal of personalities and circumstances which vary from plant to plant. Distinguishing factors almost always appear affecting the equities, in favor of or against the employee involved, such as his length of service, the manner in which he performed his regular work, the relations between the union and the employer in that particular plant, the effect of the offenses upon other employees, and other similar factors.[1]

In like manner Harry Shulman, arbitrating a discharge grievance, has contrasted the functions of adjudication under the common law and arbitration:

Generally, in sound industrial relations, technical, legalistic barriers should not be put in the way of sensible solutions deemed good for the total solution. An industrial grievance or dispute is not a negligence lawsuit where a victory is a victory regardless of the way in which it is won. An employer and the union of his employees are not litigants who meet in the courtroom and after the decision on their dispute never see each other again. The employer and the union are in continuous relations in which harmony is invaluable. They must live with each other and with the decision after the decision is made. A determination on technical legalistic grounds which do not embrace the problem to be solved may be at best fruitless and at worst the cause of greater trouble than that which it is designed to settle. Of course, specific contractual guides are binding and must be respected. But the parties should not search for wooden technicalities to gain temporary, and possibly dangerous, advantage.[2]

If the arbitration process is to be compared with any judicial process, it is the role of the chancellor in an equity proceeding that bears analogy. The analogy would apply particularly to equity proceedings in times before equity rules were crystallized into rules of precedent; when the chancellor depended chiefly upon maxims and his own conscience. Even today there is some resemblance. One arbitrator in a discipline case has observed:

[1] Feinberg, in Roberts Numbering Machine Co., 9 LA 861 (1948).

[2] Ford Motor Co. (Opinion A-31, 1943, 1 ALAA § 6,7032). Shulman and Chamberlain, *Cases on Labor Relations*, p. 464. Foundation Press (1949).

Quasi-judicial agencies such as arbiters are quite similar to courts of equity when a comparison is made of the subject matter and relief recognized and dispensed by each forum. He who comes into an arbitration proceeding asking for affirmative relief should come in with clean hands precisely as is required in a court of equity. If he does not do so, he must expect the arbiter like a chancellor to weigh the equities and offset culpabilities.[3]

But even such analogy may be misleading, especially as equity is today. Equity action is court action, based on certain accepted procedures. The occasions for equity action, its remedies, its general principles, its rules of evidence, are "law."

There is, therefore, really no "common law," in fact, no "law" of arbitration. But that does not mean that the decisions of an arbitrator are necessarily as quixotic and whimsical as those of the proverbial cadi at the gate. Certain influences may go to shape or at least circumscribe the judgment of the arbitrator, and some of them deserve mention here, because they may be called the influences of precedents in the field of arbitration.

There is first, the precedent of the contract itself. If the arbitrator feels that the terms of the collective-bargaining agreement have predetermined the issue, he would be rash to disregard it, unless he believed that he had the authority of the parties to rewrite—where, for example, they had given him a virtual carte blanche to make any reasonable decision to keep the peace and avoid a strike. Employers particularly tend to look upon arbitration as contract interpretation. The ad hoc arbitrator will be inclined to accept this view of his function, since he will normally have no reason to believe that the parties desire more of him. If the union does not subscribe to this view it would behoove it to bargain for a broader form of arbitration process, as a substitute for the strike.

Another kind of precedent that may influence the arbitrator is the prior practice of the parties themselves. The way the parties have conducted their affairs under an agreement

[3] Cheney, in Sears Roebuck & Co., 6 LA 211, 213 (1947).

is good evidence of what they meant by it. Practice may explain a contract term, or it may set it aside. Estoppel and waiver are concepts that are not peculiar to the law.

In arbitration under a permanent arbitrator or umpire, the influence of precedent comes closest to the legal rule of precedent. The umpire will tend to adhere at least to his own former decisions. Dispute settlement will develop into a pattern, handbooks promulgating these decisions will confirm the authority of precedents. If the umpire lasts long enough, he may find himself, somewhat like a judge, examining the bric-a-brac of the past, in this case his own decisions, for the answers to present problems.

The Employer's Disciplinary Powers Under Collective-Bargaining Agreements: Contract Provisions

How has the advent of unions and collective-bargaining agreements affected management's prerogative, particularly its power to discipline? Management still is able to assert its right to control and direct the working forces (that implies the power to discipline), and typically succeeds in having this prerogative inserted as an express statement in the collective-bargaining agreement. But its power is not as it was. Even if management's power to control, direct, and to discipline were not expressly curbed in the agreement, actually this power would be curbed as a practical matter. There is now in the plant a second corporate personality—a group-entity, the union.

The inclusion in a collective-bargaining agreement of reservations upon management's power to control and direct the working forces by discipline frequently represents nothing but a statement of an existing fact quite independent of the agreement—the power relationship between company and union. Realistically, therefore, it is not the collective-bargaining agreement that curbs management's prerogative. It is the organization of employees who have the right to strike. The agreement expresses the accomplished fact, and provides an orderly limitation on prerogative instead of a disorderly limitation through the employees' constant use of economic power. Even if a collective-bargaining agreement did not limit management's right to discharge for just cause only, management would in many cases not dare or even desire to discharge members of a union arbitrarily. A strike may result.

Discipline clauses in labor agreements run a range indicative of the relative bargaining positions of the parties. They vary, from clauses imposing little restraint upon management's power to discipline, to those imposing restraints of the most drastic kind. The language of these clauses should be examined carefully by company and union, to determine whether it is there by accident or design, and whether it really expresses proper discipline policy. It seems clear that when a union enters the picture, management should develop a new kind of discipline policy and should seek to effectuate it in the agreement terms. Sometimes a poor clause occurs because management lacks a sound positive policy.

In a recent study[4] of 101 collective-bargaining agreements in Indiana (of an estimated six hundred then in force) discharge provisions were analyzed as follows:

DISCHARGE PROVISIONS FOUND IN 101 AGREEMENTS

	Per Cent of 101 Agreements
Cause for Discharge:	
Just Cause Only	61
Just Cause Only—Defined	9
Violations of Company Rules & Regulations	7
List of Reasons for Discharge	5
No Mention	18
Prior Warning of Impending Discharge:	
None	74
Notice	9
Suspension	15
For Certain Offenses	2
Union's Right to Appeal Discharge:	
Granted	70
Not Mentioned	30
Time Limit on Union's Appeal	61
No Time Limit Mentioned	39

[4] Luck and Terrican, "Trends in Collective Bargaining Contracts in the State of Indiana," Indiana Business Studies, No. 31 (1950) at page 38.

It is stated that:

> Normally, a labor contract contains the provision that discharge may occur only for "just cause" or "good and sufficient" cause. More often than not, the clause is general, but sometimes the cause or causes which constitute grounds for dismissal are enumerated specifically. Since arbitration has become more common, contracts quite frequently provide that there may be no dismissal of any employee without notice to and consent of the union; and that should the union refuse its consent after having received notice, the issue is then to be presented to an arbitrator for his determination.[5]

Management sacrifices a minimum of its former legally absolute powers when it merely agrees not to be arbitrary in discharging or when the terms of the agreement impose the burden of proof upon the grievant to show that management was unreasonable. Management sacrifices a greater amount of power when it agrees not to discharge except for just cause. Management virtually surrenders its power when it agrees not to discharge, but to submit the case of a proposed discharge for consultation with the union, and failing agreement, to an arbitrator for final determination. Fortunately such clauses are rare.

Many collective-bargaining agreements may fall in between these three types, because of specific language. For example, a contract provision which has elements of types two and three is the following:

> (a) The Employer shall not discharge any permanent employee for any reason whatsoever, except such as shall be guilty of theft of goods or money. Any employee accused of and discharged for such dishonest act may, after discharge, demand and receive a hearing and decision by an arbitrator.
> (b) Notwithstanding Paragraph 6(a), it is distinctly understood that insubordination, incompetence, stalling on the job, repeated tardiness, wilful violation of reasonable working rules, insulting customers, are just cause for discharge. It is, however, distinctly understood that an employee so accused will not be discharged or dismissed from the premises until and unless the arbitrator so decides.[6]

[5] Gollub, "Discharge For Cause," Special Bulletin No. 221 (1948) Division of Research and Statistics, State of New York—Department of Labor, at page 10.

[6] Quoted in Lou Seidman & Co. (1948), 9 LA 653, 654.

Contracts such as the above seriously limit the powers of management to act in response to a situation. It may be argued that they divide responsibility and control. Management has here lost much more prerogative than in the usual case, where it reserves its right to act first, subject to the employee's subsequent right to resort to the grievance machinery. The practical consequences are great. In the usual case, the post-audit situation, not every disciplinary action will result in the filing of a grievance, nor will every sustained grievance result in the undoing of a discharge, since a discharged employee may in the meantime have obtained work elsewhere. But in the pre-audit situation, the status quo is maintained, management's hand is stayed, until the arbitrator has decided.

It may be cogently argued that such drastic restriction upon management's ability to take prompt and decisive action invites rather than cures trouble. In the words of Hill and Hook *(Management at the Bargaining Table)*:[7]

> If management is to operate its plant efficiently, it is important that it have adequate control of discipline. Discipline is not military regimentation. It is the maintenance of orderly procedures which are essential to efficient and effective production. The maintenance of discipline is the unavoidable responsibility of management. If management is to discharge its function of managing the plant it must necessarily be in a position to maintain discipline—a prerequisite to orderly production. If management seeks participation by the union in the maintenance of discipline, management runs the danger of losing its right to handle the discipline problem promptly and effectively, thereby limiting its ability to maintain discipline.
>
> The following considerations should be given great weight in arriving at a sound management position on the question of discipline in an industrial organization:
>
> 1. Management has the unquestioned responsibility of maintaining discipline and must be free to exercise its best discretion in doing so. It must be free to take prompt action to remove the cause of any interference with discipline. Accordingly, management should not share its disciplinary authority with anyone else.
> 2. However, disciplinary action should be for cause. To prevent arbitrary disciplinary measures, evidence of cause may be questioned through the grievance procedure.

[7] At page 90.

3. The making of disciplinary action subject to the grievance procedure should not be allowed to interfere with management's right to remove an employee from his place of work, in case of breach of discipline. Management must be free to take appropriate action immediately.

Pre-audit procedure provisions may be opposed by management for reasons such as the above. A provision which would tie management's hands and require arbitration before disciplinary action could effectively be taken would destroy much of the value of discipline. It does not necessarily follow, however, that management should oppose a provision which curbs its power to discharge an employee by requiring an arbitrator to pass on the question before a discharge would be effective, provided that the employer retains the power to suspend the employee and take him off the job pending the determination of the grievance. Such provision does not strip management of effective disciplinary power. It can still meet a given situation by immediate action.

To what extent should a company consult with the union before taking disciplinary action, as a matter of policy, rather than obligation? In some cases it may be advisable to talk matters over with the union before drastic action is taken. Management should do its best to appear reasonable and considerate. To keep the union advised is one thing; to consult with it is another. And to expect or even ask the union to adhere to management's suggestions as to the need for disciplining a particular worker, and the extent of the discipline to be imposed, is unrealistic. A union is not in business to approve such things as discharges, even inferentially.

It has been suggested that management should make freer use in disciplinary problems of the grievance procedure—to protest as a complainant through the various steps of the grievance procedure the conduct of particular employees. In one case, an arbitrator, commenting upon deficiencies in company-union relations in a particular plant, quoted with approval from a Bulletin of the Division of Labor Standards of the United States Department of Labor:

Collective bargaining is a two-way street and management may at times have just cause for bringing complaints against the union or against an individual employee. Sometimes management complains that the grievance machinery seems to be designed exclusively for the benefit of the union since the workers make all the complaints. Where such a situation exists it is usually because management puts through a discharge or other disciplinary action without prior consultation.

Many grievances of this sort could be avoided by prior complaints to the union about the conduct of a worker which may seem to call for disciplinary action. In this way, the union shares the responsibility for whatever action is taken instead of merely playing the role of critic.

Some contracts make specific provision for procedure in cases of management grievances. Even where such a provision is not actually written into the contract, the grievance procedure works best when union representatives and employees remember that they are both partners to the bargain.

Just as the freest possible interpretation of what is a worker's legitimate grievance helps to eliminate all causes of resentment, real or imaginary, so management's right to present a grievance helps the union to recognize and modify those of its practices (or the employee's) which cause management unnecessary inconvenience. The great advantage of such a free exchange of criticism is that management and the union can discover unhealthy conditions more quickly and in many cases can remedy such conditions before a grievance is actually presented.[8]

The advice given in the above quotation may be inappropriate to many situations. It may be properly followed where management's objective is merely to warn an employee, and have the justice of the warning, and the effectiveness of it, conceded by a union or approved by an arbitrator. But appearing as a grievant is hardly the proper role of management if it decides that discipline should take the form of action, rather than words.

Management, which bears the responsibility of maintaining order, must see that the authority which should accompany that responsibility remains an effective force.

The Arbitrator

It is of the essence of collective bargaining with regard to

[8] International Minerals and Chemical Corp., 4 LA 127 (1946) at page 130. (Quoting from Bulletin No. 60, page 6.)

management's disciplinary powers that certain procedures be established for the handling of grievances in disciplinary matters. Sometimes these procedures are simply the grievance procedures established for the handling of all disputes between management and union as to the application of the collective-bargaining agreement. Sometimes special procedures for disciplinary grievances are established (e.g., special provisions re notice, hearing, etc.).

If the processes of continuous collective bargaining and resort to intermediate stages of the grievance procedure fail, collective-bargaining agreements typically provide that an arbitrator shall act as *deus ex machina,* the great reconciler, permanent or ad hoc, to decide when discipline is fair and proper. Thus the prerogatives formerly exclusively exercised by management are now to that extent shared with the arbitrator. He is given the power because the parties have failed to agree, and because they prefer to have him decide rather than resort to economic force. His judgment is the second best thing: The fundamental need, even when there is an arbitrator, is for union and management to agree if they can.

What kind of person is this arbitrator likely to be? He must be one who knows that management is not always right and not always wrong, and that labor is not always right and not always wrong. In all probability this middle-of-the-road viewpoint has already been manifested in his prior decisions. The word has got around. He has not (at least not yet) been blacklisted by either camp. He is a balance-wheeler. He is probably a man who abhors extra-legal force. He is probably an educated man—chances are great that he is either a lawyer, or a college professor of economics, industry, sociology, or political science, acquainted, at least in an academic way, with business activities. He has probably had some experience in government—most likely with the War Labor Board. In his personal life he tries to keep up appearances, and is not given to associating with ruffians or breakers of the law, high or low. He is probably a middleclasser. As such, he may have developed an attitude which operates in the atmosphere of public policy.

Into the hands of this semi-realist, semi-idealist, the parties have, for want of better, committed much responsibility. He has the disadvantage of one who has usually experienced only vicariously—he does not know what really happened, but only what the parties desired to or succeeded in telling him. But this remarkable fellow is a kind of brooding presence, a super-conscience, in every union-organized factory. Management's disciplinary prerogatives and union's job security are alike tested in the actualities of his utterances. While he sits the functions of management are suspended. Management becomes the pleader, not the judge. In many of their dealings with one another with regard to discipline, management and union are guessing on what he will decide. Right is tested in the crucible of his court of appeals (though might, i.e., bargaining power, is always in the background). He assumes the mantle of responsibility as the Decision-maker.

With little or no guide furnished by the parties as to what standards the arbitrator is to apply in disciplinary cases (what is just cause?) he is frequently required to draw upon general concepts of justice and fairness. Experienced arbitrators with a philosophic, introspective turn of mind may well reflect dubiously upon the highly personalized character of a decision on a disciplinary problem. Since *stare decisis* is meaningless, particularly in ad hoc arbitrations, he cannot simply grasp the helping hand of precedent or merely lean upon the crutch of someone else's decision. The permanent arbitrator may be somewhat better off than the ad hoc arbitrator in this respect. The permanent arbitrator especially does have the guide of grievance settlements by the parties themselves, as well as previous disciplines not appealed by the union, and does strive to fit the decisions, in the case before him, to the pattern of equity as conceived by the parties. But all in all, the arbitrator must make up his mind for himself. What he decides, his attitude toward disciplinary problems, will tend to be influenced by all the things that have gone to make up his composite sense of morality and fair play. The ethical teachings of his parents, religious advisers, the stereotypes of his friends, particularly in younger days when his mind was plastic, may subtly guide his thinking. His experiences and attitudes toward life, be they hard or soft, may condition him in favor of or against toleration of particular offenses, and motivate him for or against mercy or rigor. The mores of his present environment, the thinking of his present associates, may also be influential. These basic attitudes must remain unproven assumptions, since they rarely, if at all, find expression in his opinions, which will speak unemotionally and objectively. But they may play their role particularly in his weighing of the facts, in his evaluation of the proof. "An arbitrator's lot is not a happy one."

The vagueness of the standards he has to go by—the fact that in a collective-bargaining agreement the parties have really agreed to defer agreement on management's disciplinary prerogative—especially tempt him to the personalized decision. That is the human factor in arbitration, and the task of the arbitrator is to minimize it.

The Arbitrator and "Just Cause"

The just arbitrator, like the just judge, must strive to rise above himself. He must make an impersonal decision and render an award founded, if possible, upon more objective criteria, consonant with the will of the parties, and expressive of wider concepts of justice than his own private opinions. One arbitrator, grappling with the task before him, declared:

> It is ordinarily the function of an Arbitrator in interpreting a contract provision which requires "sufficient cause" as a condition precedent to discharge not only to determine whether the employee involved is guilty of wrongdoing and, if so, to confirm the employer's right to discipline where its exercise is essential to the objective of efficiency, but also to safeguard the interests of the discharged employee by making reasonably sure that the causes for discharge were just and equitable and such as would appeal to reasonable and fair-minded persons as warranting discharge. To be sure, no standards exist to aid an Arbitrator in

finding a conclusive answer to such a question, and, therefore, perhaps the best he can do is to decide what a reasonable man, mindful of the habits and customs of industrial life and of the standards of justice and fair dealing prevalent in the community ought to have done under similar circumstances and in that light to decide whether the conduct of the discharged employee was defensible and the disciplinary penalty just.[9]

Few, if any, men can afford to dissociate themselves from their environment; least of all can decision-makers in human relations spurn prevalent attitude and custom. The arbitrator must try to cast aside his idiosyncrasies and make a decision that harmonizes with what are then considered to be enlightened concepts of justice. It is the rule of the arbitrator, as it is of the judge, to be as objective as possible. Thus only can he hope to approximate what the parties had in mind when they asked him to decide the case. In a certain sense, he should be the spokesman for his day and age in the field of industrial relations. He should try to keep under control the tempting tendency to make visceral decisions of personal preference. Few thinking men would claim that they are so composed that their own emotional likes and dislikes may not sneak into their most judicious decisions. But it is a question of degree; there is such a thing as being aware of the danger and guarding against it.

Frequently the arbitrator, striving to achieve the impersonal, the demonstrably fair decision in a disciplinary case, must feel baffled by the fact that the parties have given him so little guide in the contract. When company and union agree that discharge (and frequently other disciplinary action) shall be only for "just cause" or words of similar import, they have hardly agreed to anything currently, except to work out future disputes on disciplinary action amicably through continuous collective bargaining and through use of the grievance procedure. In the words of George W. Taylor:

What has actually been agreed upon? No understanding has been reached about the limits of proper and necessary discipline, but

[9] Platt and Lavery, in Riley Stoker Corp., 7 LA, 765, 767 (1947).

there is established a procedure for gradually arriving at such an understanding. The agreement of the parties with respect to discipline will gradually be filled out as management action in some cases is accepted as reasonable and as union protests over other disciplinary cases are settled through the grievance procedure. The term "for cause" will gradually acquire meaning.

Under the identical clause, entirely different understandings about disciplinary powers have been developed in various plants. In some cases management's discipline power has been virtually eliminated; in others it remains stern and rigid. In view of this experience it is pertinent to ask, where is the vital agreement of the parties made as respects discipline—in the labor contract or in the handling of grievances?[10]

One arbitrator, wisely seeking an objective approach to deciding a discipline problem, observed:

About all that an impartial arbitrator can do, therefore, is to decide the justice or injustice of the discharge here in question, in the light of (a) common sense, (b) common knowledge of generally prevailing industry standards for employee deportment, and (c) common understanding and when—*absent specific criteria mutually agreed*—an employer may fairly and justly discharge an employee with seniority rights.[11]

Granted; but what do these words mean?

The arbitrator may sometimes wonder: What approach to the discipline problem do the parties really want? They may manifest a complete disagreement. Would they not be better off if they tried to define a little more distinctly the attributes of this "just cause" they so glibly refer to in the collective bargaining agreement?

In their attitude toward "just cause," arbitrators vary exceedingly. In one camp may be found those who seem inclined to uphold the management prerogative; who seem to feel that reasons of policy and contract interpretation require that a measure of discretion, freedom in fact-finding and applying the penalty, must be accorded management. They are inclined to emphasize the preventive purposes of disciplinary action; to emphasize concepts like "normal" standards of behavior, and to take cognizance of them. In

[10] 26 Personnel. 236 (1949). (American Management Association, Inc.)
[11] Tyree, in Campbell Soup Co., 10 LA 207, 208 (1948).

another camp may be found arbitrators who are not so much interested in the company prerogative approach as they are in an industrial relations approach. They are sensitive to the impact of drastic discipline upon the individual worker, inclined to feel that job security is usually more important than prevention by strong measures. Thinking in terms of the industrial worker, they dislike sending him home to a needy family without a job. To them, discharge is truly the capital punishment of industrial relations, and they share with certain criminologists distaste for capital punishment. Actually, however, many arbitrators will have no consistent policy, but will emphasize one approach or the other in accordance with their reaction to specific cases.

According to Cleeton, *(The New Approach to Employee Discipline)* employee discipline in America has passed through three stages:

> The first can best be described as the "Mailed-Fist Era." The underlying philosophy seems to have been "Treat 'em rough and make 'em like it." The methods were dictatorial and militaristic. This style of employee management became almost extinct following the first World War.
>
> The second may be designated as the "Rules and Regulations Era." The philosophy and method were distinctly legalistic, and the objective was to make employee management routine and systematic. This viewpoint grew out of efforts to put personnel management on an efficiency basis. The motives were laudable, but results were often disappointing.
>
> The new approach to discipline is individualistic in philosophy and clinical in method.[12]

This clinical approach to discipline (the industrial relations approach popular with many arbitrators) tends to view discharge as a measure of last resort. Men, like materials, should be scrapped only when there is no salvage value in them. The approach calls for inquiry into the causes accounting for the discipline problem in question. Proper analysis of such causes, it is felt, will yield values in determining whether the employee has fundamental, non-salvageable personality faults or whether certain corrective measures in

[12] 16 Personnel. 197 (1940). (American Management Association, Inc.)

plant management or in the personal conduct of the employee will give promise of preventing repetition of the problem.

In determining whether just cause exists for discharge or other diciplinary action, many arbitrators accordingly have used no slot-machine mechanical approach. Instead, they have become balancers of equities. They have sifted many pros and cons. Among the inquiries that have been recognized as bearing on "just cause" are: (a) How serious is the offense, considering the job and the practice in the plant? (b) Has management contributed to the commission of the offense by such things as faulty instruction, supervision, condonation of similar offenses? (c) Does the offense characterize the offender, or do past record, temporary personal difficulties, an amenable attitude, indicate that the employee deserves special consideration?

These, among others, are factors frequently noticed by arbitrators of discipline disputes. The problem is to achieve flexibility without sacrifice of basic consistency. To those who feel that the offense must be defined in the light of the surrounding circumstances, consistency does not require that all offenders should be treated alike, without regard to the above considerations.

If industrial discipline is to achieve its purpose and promote efficiency, it must appeal to the sense of fairness of the employees, whose morale is important:

> Arbitrator is aware that, in order to operate the laboratory efficiently, attendance must be steady and work must be performed properly and reasonable decorum practiced; also that occasional discipline for avoidable offenses is warranted and helpful to both company and workers so long as this discipline is not imposed in an unreasonable manner and is recognized as just and fair by the staff generally. Any discipline that is deemed as vindictive or biased results in the action having the opposite effect, and, in line with these thoughts and the claim by the company that it seeks to enjoy at all times the good will of the workers and the union, the arbitrator believes that this discharge cannot be classed as being for "just cause."[13]

[13] Copelof, in Precision Film Laboratories, Inc., 3 LA 538, 541 (1946).

To provide that an employee shall be discharged only for "just cause" is, like so many other well-rounded phrases, merely the beginning, rather than the end of the inquiry. "It is one of those provisions which will have to get meaning and context by a process of inclusion and exclusion of particular situations as these arise." It is like the legal phrases "reasonable care," "scope of employment," "due process," etc.—an open invitation to inquire into the facts of each case.

It is sometimes difficult to know where to stop:

> When an employee alleges that he was discharged or penalized without good cause, he places at issue not only his own conduct, but that of the employer, as well. Present in every such case is the question of whether or not the employer was properly exercising his disciplinary functions under the Agreement. The Umpire must ask not only, "What did Employee X do?" but also, such questions as, "What did Management do to warn and correct him? Did Management treat other employees, similarly situated, in the same way? In the last analysis, and under all the circumstances, was Management fair?" Those inquiries have constantly been pursued by the Umpire in discipline cases. Only when they were answered has the Umpire been able to decide whether Management's exercise of its right to discipline for cause was proper and should be upheld.[14]

Even the clinical approach may be overdone, if it results in too much concentration on the problems of the individual employee, without reference to other considerations. For example, there is the fact that the collective-bargaining agreement and the prior practice of the parties must be taken into account. If the parties have definitely agreed upon a certain treatment for a particular offense ("price lists"), there is little room, if any, for a clinical approach which would be contrary to that agreement. Absent specific agreement, and sometimes in spite of agreement, past practice may be the guide to the solution of the problem. Past practice may be the best evidence of the parties' ideas of just discipline under the circumstances. If a decision does not conform to past practice, it can create chaos in the plant.

[14] Seward, in Matter of General Motors Corp. and U.A.W. decided September 5, 1944, quoted by McCoy, U.S. Pipe & Foundry Co., 10 LA 48, 49 (1948).

There is also the relation of discipline to plant need. Harshness, rather than mercy, may be indicated in particular cases because plant need requires it. There are occasions when strong measures are required—somewhat like the "clear and present danger" test. Discipline is sometimes not merely an individual matter. It can create a precedent, establish a pattern. It may be useful as a warning to other employees to watch their conduct. Often group good seems to conflict with individual good. If he is to resolve the dilemma properly, the arbitrator must be truly a wise man. For arbitration is more of an art than a science.

The arbitrator must further bear in mind that he is part of a process whereby the parties hope to achieve a sound industrial relationship. He has a right to assume, at least where the contract does not speak clearly to the contrary, that the workable, practical result is the one of the parties bargained for. He should question any proposal that he decide in a way that fails to effectuate a harmonious efficient relationship between the parties. Of course there may be times when an arbitrator feels compelled to make an award which may be intolerable for the parties to live under—an award which demands negotiation leading to contract amendment—let the chips fall where they may. The ad hoc arbitrator in particular may have to face up to this situation. But frequently the arbitrator will find upon fuller consideration that the workable decision, the one in keeping with sound industrial relations, is also the more reasonable one, the one more consonant with the total meaning of the contract under which he arbitrates.

What, then, is just cause? The arbitrator frequently finds himself pulled in different directions by varying approaches and considerations, which may logically bear upon the question he has to decide. Somehow or other he must decide the case, strike the practical equation, though philosophers blanch. But he should not really be ashamed if he cannot say what "just cause" as a concept is, if he can merely grope toward an answer in each case as it comes along. The question of "just cause" is nothing less than the question of justice, placed in an industrial setting. True, it is not legal justice, criminal or civil; it is not divine justice; it is not social justice—it is industrial justice. Its attributes are not for that fact more easily defined. The question, What is justice? (like the kindred question, What is truth?) has troubled the world's greatest philosophers, from Plato to the present. The things that have vexed the philosophers also vex the arbitrators, though these practitioners may not theorize. When the arbitrator is confronted with the basic, irreducible question, he will find that advice, experience, knowledge, even intelligence, will avail little, if he does not possess the God-given faculty of wisdom to guide him to the right result. There is no substitute for that.

Proving the Facts

In addition to their general power to define "just cause" and to apply the concept to a given situation, arbitrators have asserted two very important ancillary powers: (1) the power to establish standards of proof and evidence, and (2) the power to review the propriety of the particular penalty imposed—in other words, the power to modify, and not simply to uphold or reverse the employer's action.

First, with regard to matters of proof. It goes virtually without saying that many claims stand or fall upon the question of burden of proof. Half the world goes round on lack of proof. Fortunes are made and lost on lack of proof. When arbitrators rule, as they usually do, that the company has the burden of proof to show that the grievant was discharged or otherwise disciplined for just cause, they are telling the employer that he must sweat uphill or lose. For management action is under scrutiny.

Blindfolded Justice cannot decide for him unless he tips the scales by evidence—evidence he can bring forth at the hearing, not just confidential evidence in his files. He will find that it is not advisable to use many potential witnesses, co-worker informants who don't mind telling him privately what happened but who implore him not to call them as stool pigeons to the witness stand. If he does call them, they may reverse themselves.

By and large, his witnesses are limited to his foremen and other supervisory employees. At least he can depend on their loyalty. But their testimony may be weak and second-rate, especially if they have not personally seen or heard, smelt, felt, or tasted the fact in question. And even when they are competent to testify, it makes the arbitration hearing very costly, to have high-priced personnel sitting around waiting to testify, getting paid for taking the day off. He wonders, is it worth it?

The employer may think the arbitrator somewhat unreasonable in his unwillingness to draw "logical conclusions." Arbitrators generally take a dim view of so-called circumstantial evidence. They may refuse to presume that negligence caused a certain accident from the fact that most accidents of that kind do not happen without negligence. But how can one actually prove negligence in a certain case, if the only witness to the accident, the only one who knows what really happened, is the suspected culprit himself? (There is, of course, a question whether discipline should be invoked by management in such case even if there is no union.)

Then there are the physical difficulties of assembling the detailed proof that may be necessary to show things like unsatisfactory course of conduct as the basis of discharge. Inefficiency, failure to meet production standards, unwillingness to coöperate—charges constituting the accumulation of acts or omissions severally petty in themselves, serious in the aggregate—may require for proof a convincing array of records or remembered incidents. The evidence of the company may not be up to this requirement. Sniping tactics of the opposition may deflate the testimony, may confuse the arbitrator until he wonders whether the grievant is the persecuted victim of trivialities. Records are so easily kept poorly. The production standards of the company may not stand the test of cross-examination: they may be assailed as management's dream of utopia rather than realistic yardsticks of efficiency. Charges that the grievant is a "bad actor," uncoöperative, may be met in the best defensive style by counter-charges that the foreman has a psychopathic dislike for the grievant, that there is a clash of personalities, discrimination, and so forth. There is no telling what the outcome will be.

Special difficulty may be encountered in proving charges of dishonesty. In effect, the company is asking the arbitrator to find that the employee is a criminal. Naturally, the arbitrator will want to be given strong proof. To sustain a discharge may be to condemn the grievant permanently to the ranks of the unemployed. In a case like this the arbitrator sometimes finds his sense of justice at war with itself, and he may fervently regret that he assumed the obligation to arbitrate the grievance.

Let one not suppose, however, that the union, in representing the grievant, does not have its own problems of proof. Often the union faces the necessity of meeting the company's evidence by evidence of its own—to bear the burden of rebuttal. The union too may be frustrated in its endeavor to convert suspicion into fact. There is sometimes the tantalizing feeling that there is much evidence, favorable to the grievant, in company records or known by the company officials, which cannot be pried loose. When the union flails around and charges discrimination in a particular case, sometimes it is merely trying to throw dust in the arbitrator's eyes; but sometimes, no doubt, if the truth were known, the truth would support the charge. But how to prove it?

Indeed, in this matter of proof, both company and union are confronted with fundamental uncertainties. There are the uncertainties of collecting and presenting the evidence. There are the uncertainties of the attitudes of arbitrators toward evidence painfully collected and presented. Notwithstanding apparent similarity of rulings by many arbitrators on evidence and burden of proof, their agreement may be only skin deep. For evaluation of evidence is personalized. And the same arbitrator may view and weigh evidence differently in different cases. The kind of offense involved and the kind of penalty imposed may go to vary the weight of the evidence. The more serious the charge, the more serious may be the proof that an arbitrator will require to sustain it. The kind of activity involved may be important. In railroad cases, arbitrators have imposed the burden of proof upon the grievant. The heavy public responsibilities of transportation companies may disincline arbitrators to meddle too much in the administration of discipline. The previous record of the employee may affect the burden of proof. All in all, the quantum of evidence, like the interpretation of evidence, may turn out to be extremely variable.

To discipline policy has been added the unknown x factor—x being the amount of evidence sufficient to satisfy the arbitrator who may have to decide the ensuing grievance. Companies may risk its absence, and gamble. But to others the watchword may be caution. It would be natural for employers, though convinced that they have just cause, to hesitate to discipline employees unless the x factor is present. Old timers in the executive force may ruefully observe, "we have a stranger in our midst."

In the arbitration of discipline problems, as in problems of justice generally, there may be a vast disparity between proof and reality. As he hears the evidence of witnesses pro and con, the sensitive arbitrator, like the sensitive judge, cannot help but feel that sometimes the similarity (if any) between the story told and actual events and persons is purely coincidental. Justice is an art, and like other arts, requires assumptions. The scenery of the stage taxes credibility no more sometimes than the testimony of witnesses who swear to tell the truth, the whole truth, and nothing but the truth.

From a pragmatic point of view, the function of the arbitrator is not to dispense ideal justice, but to do justice according to the evidence before him. Company and union must appreciate that what they know and what they can make the arbitrator know are often two different things. If ideal justice is not accomplished, the fault may be the arbitrator's.

The arbitrator who is in the middle of skirmishing over

proof cannot but resent being made the dupe, when he senses a desire on one or both sides to win the case regardless of the consequences. Employers and unions who win cases they should not win, because facts are misrepresented or concealed, win hollow victories. Such victories may in the long run poison their relations. For good industrial relations are built on frankness and fairness.

The Penalty

In a second important way, arbitrators have accepted control over the employer's disciplinary power: they have generally asserted the right to pass not merely upon the cause for disciplinary action, but also upon the propriety of the particular penalty imposed. Granted that the employee committed an act warranting disciplinary measures, was the particular degree of discipline justified?

This is the question: Should arbitrators substitute their own judgment as to the appropriateness of penalty for that of the company? Naturally, management frequently answers an emphatic "No!" To establish cause for discipline, it is contended, is a severe enough burden. To require the company also to demonstrate its fairness in selecting a particular form of discipline taxes the fact-proving ability of management unduly.

Most arbitrators seem to feel that, absent contract provisions to the contrary, there is no halfway point at which they can stop in the determination of "just cause." If "just cause" may question the factual basis of the employer's action it may also question the kind of action he took.

The power to review the penalty has been variously claimed on a wide or limited basis. A cautious arbitrator (of the limited basis school of thought) has said:

> Where an employee has violated a rule or engaged in conduct meriting disciplinary action, it is primarily the function of management to decide upon the proper penalty. If management acts in good faith upon a fair investigation and fixes a penalty not inconsistent with that imposed in other like cases, an arbitrator should not disturb it. The mere fact that management has im-

posed a somewhat different penalty than the arbitrator would have, if he had had the decision to make originally, is no justification for changing it. The minds of equally reasonable men differ. A consideration which would weigh heavily with one man will seem of less importance to another. A circumstance which highly aggravates an offense in one man's eyes may be only slight aggravation to another. If an arbitrator could substitute his judgment and discretion for the judgment and discretion honestly exercised by management, then the functions of management would have been abdicated, and unions would take every case to arbitration. The result would be as intolerable to employees as to management. The only circumstance under which a penalty imposed by management can be rightfully set aside by an arbitrator are those where discrimination, unfairness, or capricious and arbitrary action are proved—in other words, where there has been abuse of discretion.[15]

A wider basis for review has frequently been asserted:

In many disciplinary cases, the reasonableness of the penalty imposed on an employee rather than the existence of proper cause for disciplining him is the question an arbitrator must decide. This is not so under contracts or submission agreements which expressly prohibit an arbitrator from modifying or reducing a penalty if he finds that disciplinary action was justified, but most current labor agreements do not contain such limiting clause. In disciplinary cases generally, therefore, most arbitrators exercise the right to change or modify a penalty if it is found to be improper or too severe, under all the circumstances of the situation. This right is deemed to be inherent in the arbitrator's power to decide the sufficiency of the cause for discipline and in his authority to finally settle and adjust the dispute before him. In deciding the reasonableness of the penalty imposed or whether it should be modified, arbitrators take into consideration many important factors. In the first place, it is not socially desirable that disciplinary penalties for industrial offenses be regarded strictly as punishment for wrongdoing. Rather, the object of the penalty should be to make employees recognize their responsibilities so that they might become better workers in the future. Where, therefore, disciplinary action is justified, but discharge is deemed too severe a penalty, an arbitrator may consider what lesser penalty would be fair and just in the circumstances. . . .

[15] McCoy, in Standard Oil Co. of Indiana, 1 LA 159, 162 (1946).

In a word, do justice and fair dealing warrant a reduction in his penalty?[16]

Another arbitrator has expressed the thought somewhat similarly:

> . . . the situation may well arise where the disciplinary action is onerous and excessive. And if it be so, then it well behooves an Umpire to consider the penalty in its relation to the offense and adjust it commensurately. It is a basic principle of equity that the penalty must bear reasonable relationship to the offense involved. That is simple justice.[17]

The Arbitrator has thus contributed to a reëxamination of discipline techniques in unionized industrial establishments. He has expressed not merely current thinking on the theory of industrial discipline. His strategic position has enabled him to influence the actual process. His judgments become the criteria to which personnel directors must look to avoid loss of prestige. Let us consider what attitude arbitrators have taken toward various industrial penalties.

(A) The Penalty of Discharge

(With Some Treatment of Reinstatement, with or without Back Pay)

Discharge is viewed as a measure of last resort. If there is one generalization that can safely be made from examination of arbitration reports, it is that arbitrators typically are loath to uphold discharges. To say that discharge is the capital punishment of industry is accepted parlance. Particularly for a first offense, a flagrant case is required, if a discharge is to be sustained:

> It is very seldom that the first infraction of a rule or the first insubordinate act by an employee is considered proper grounds

[16] Harry Platt, "The Arbitration Process in the Settlement of Labor Disputes," *Journal of the American Judicature Society*, August 1947, pp. 54-60, at p. 58. Published by the American Judicature Society, Hutchins Hall, Ann Arbor, Michigan. Quoted by Hepburn in E. I. Dupont de Nemours & Co., Inc. 9 LA 345, 348 (1947).

[17] Shipman, in Bethlehem Steel Co. 9 LA 954, 955 (1948).

for discharge. Discharge is the maximum penalty which can be imposed in disciplinary cases and is not normally imposed on first offenders. It should be noted that there was no evidence of any previous rule infraction or insubordination on the part of Graham. . . .[18]

The usual importance of previous warning, particularly written warning, before taking the drastic action of discharge, is frequently recognized:

A warning system has several purposes. On the one hand, it puts the employee on notice that the Company takes a serious view of his behavior and the repetition thereof will lead to discharge. On the other hand, it focuses attention clearly on the particular behavior of which the Company complains; if the employee feels the warning unjustified, he may resort to the grievance procedure in order to clear himself. At the very least, such recourse permits a finding of the facts when they are still fresh in the people's minds. Miller conceded that he had on various occasions received verbal "spankings" from supervisors, but these are not the same as written warnings. . . .[19]

While affirming the company's right to discharge in proper cases, arbitrators frequently find reasons not to uphold it in the present one. Even "dubious equities" may sway the arbitrator toward mercy.

Despite the fact that the employee here concerned was undoubtedly guilty of wrongdoing of two kinds just before his discharge, the arbitrator feels that there are some factors in the case which tend to make the extreme act of discharge somewhat severe. The Company had not by publication of any rule clarified its contention that it is the duty of all foremen to enforce all general rules and the duty of all other employees to obey foremen in respect to orders concerning them. It is true that it can be argued with great force that every employee with ordinary common sense should know it to be his duty to obey all rules called to his attention by any supervisors; yet the present custom of making these matters clear and explicit by bulletin board publication and the fact that no notice supporting the company's contention had been published in the plant tend to create some dubious equities in favor of the employee here concerned. . . .[20]

[18] Whiting, in WLEU Broadcasting Co., 7 LA 151, 153 (1947).
[19] Stein, in Pyrene Mfg. Co., 9 LA 787, 788 (1948).
[20] Updegraff, in John Deere Tractor Co., 4 LA 161, 163 (1946).

Remedially minded arbitrators may in general be quite justified in their distaste for discharge; and it may not prove any point to cite instances where their mercy to the employee seems to have been merciless to the employer. But where arbitrators have been willing to reinstate flagrant trouble makers, particularly those who have retaliated against disliked supervisors by beating them up (Should it really matter whether the assault occurs on or off the premises?) one may wonder whether certain decisions reduce the employer's discharge power to plus or minus zero.

The reluctance of arbitrators to find "just cause" for discharge may result in attempts to place new employees on a probationary status beyond the normal protections of the collective-bargaining agreement. One arbitrator in a discipline case has commented:

> A trial period is particularly important in office work to determine whether a new employee has the capacity and personality to perform the variety of functions which may be assigned. Office work is not so standardized or simplified as most manual work, and a substantial probationary period is required if an efficient and capable working force is to be maintained or developed.[21]

In another dispute, an arbitrator found that where the parties had in practice (though not in their contract) recognized a probationary status for the first thirty days of employment, the employer had "wider latitude" to discharge during this period than thereafter. It was stated:

> A probationary period is desirable and in fact necessary to protect both the employer and the employee. Without it, there would be no way to select new employees and determine their fitness. Once employed, even for a day, they could not be discharged except "for proper cause," subject to appeal. In the absence of a probationary period, the cause for discharge must be more liberally construed than in the case of the discharge of experienced employees. The employer must be given greater leeway or else the employment process could result in fastening on the employment rolls and on the seniority rolls incompetent employees who would have been weeded out in the normal operation of probation in the first days of work.[22]

[21] Kerr, in Luckenbach Steamship Co., Inc. 6 LA 98, 102 (1946).
[22] Lapp, in Park Sherman Co., 2 LA 199, 200 (1946).

One cannot comment upon the arbitrator's review of discharge grievances without dwelling upon his power to reinstate. When collective-bargaining agreements gave arbitrators power to reinstate discharged employees, a revolution in industrial relations was effected. No power of the arbitrator more than this highlights the change away from the employer's former absolute power to direct the working forces. The employer can no longer say to his discharged employee, "So what—sue me!" Now, like it or not, he may have to take the employee back. The frequency with which arbitrators have exercised their power to reinstate indicates the decisiveness of the change.

The arbitrator may qualify his order to reinstate. He may try to play policeman over the employee's future conduct. A familiar instance occurs where the arbitrator warns the employee that any repetition of his misconduct will justify discipline. Arbitral warning may be particularly effective where the arbitrator is permanent, as distinguished from ad hoc. Sometimes the arbitrator goes further, and asserts authority to secure future good conduct by placing the employee on probation.

Occasionally an arbitrator asserts the anomalous power of sustaining the discharge and ordering the employer to reinstate the grievant as a new employee. One suspects that in so doing he is trying to divide the baby in dead center. The result may be loss of all benefits accrued from prior service. To decide that an employer has a right to discharge an employee and at the same time a duty to reëmploy him seems illogical, however much the ruling may accomplish rough justice in a particular case.

Accompanying the power to reinstate is usually the power to award or to deny back pay for the period of unemployment. When arbitrators feel that the employee has committed an offense not serious enough to warrant discharge but serious enough to warrant a suspension they may deny some or all of the claim for back pay.

Many arbitration awards in discharge cases have ordered reinstatement without back pay or with back pay for only a part of the period involved. This is proper where the employee has been guilty of fault, but discharge is considered too severe a penalty in the light of past practices, etc., and the award in effect, if not in precise words, changes the discharge to a disciplinary lay-off. . . .[23]

The arbitrator must frame his back-pay award carefully. If he grants full back pay, he should beware lest he unconsciously overdo it. Account should be taken of unemployment compensation benefits the grievant may have received, or wages received from interim employment.

Some questions that may arise concerning the proper measure of the back-pay allowance are: (1) Does a discharged employee, appealing his discharge through arbitration proceedings, have a duty to seek employment to mitigate damages, to minimize a back-pay award in case he is reinstated? The question is rarely raised: apparently management does not expect it of him. Arbitrators have not imposed such a duty upon him. A common law court might hold otherwise. (2) Should the award include overtime pay that the employee might have earned, had he not been wrongfully discharged? One arbitrator has ruled:

Ordinarily such pay would be denied on the ground that the matter is purely conjectural. In this case it is not conjectural. By the Company's own admission Wansley would have been required to work, and would have been subject to discipline had he refused.[24]

The arbitrator also pointed out that his substitute had worked overtime, and concluded "the facts removed the matter entirely from the field of conjecture." He criticized the ruling of another arbitrator:

The arbitrator . . . in awarding compensation denied them the shift differential. In this denial, I think that the arbitrator lost sight of the theory of compensation, namely, of making the employee whole. . . . If the inconvenience of working at night were a sound reason for deducting compensation, then it might just as logically be argued that no compensation should be paid.[25]

[23] McCoy in Masonite Corp., 10 LA 854, 857 (1948).
[24] *Ibid.* at 856.
[25] *Ibid.* at 856.

(3) Should the employee's refusal to accept other work in the plant bar his claim for back pay, in the event that his discharge is held to be improper? Here we have a situation which has persuaded more than one arbitrator to deny back pay to the grievant. (Note that the question here is not whether the employee had a duty to seek, but rather whether he had a right to refuse, proffered employment).

(B) SUSPENSION OR LAYOFF

A form of remedy more in favor with arbitrators than discharge, because it lacks its final and irremediable character, is the disciplinary layoff. The power to suspend for breach of discipline has been recognized as an implied power of management. In one case, the union argued that the terms of the collective-bargaining agreement in question should be construed to prohibit the employer from imposing layoff as a form of discipline. This contention was denied by the arbitrator, who said:

> The argument of the Union, with respect to this article of the contract, is that the term "lay-off" means "lay-off because of curtailment of forces." There is no evidence whatever that when the parties wrote the contract they intended to thus limit the meaning of that term. The disciplinary lay-off is in such constant and practically universal use throughout the country that I would be entirely unjustified in narrowing the meaning of the term "lay-off" so as to exclude the disciplinary lay-off. The Arbitration Reports are full of cases which show that the disciplinary lay-off is a common form of penalty. I have seen no case where it has been held that the Company has no right to use such form of penalty, except where the contract expressly forbids it. See matter of Masonite Corporation, 10 L A 854, where there was such an express provision. . . .[26]

The real question in a disciplinary layoff grievance is whether the particular facts justify the penalty. The penalty may be challenged as too severe under the circumstances. Frequently arbitrators have reduced or set aside suspension when they thought company action too severe. The attitude

[26] McCoy in Koppers Co., Inc., 11 LA 334, 335 (1948).

of some of them is consonant with the advice of Pigors and Myers:

Disciplinary lay offs, in fact, have probably been used too readily, especially in periods of labor surplus. One old-time supervisor admitted this in discussions leading to the formulation of a new disciplinary policy, when he said, "the fellow you lay off is often glad to take the time off, and in the meantime you've lost the services of one of your regular hands. And, if he isn't glad for the loaf, he's sore at you when he is allowed to come back."[27]

When arbitrators reinstate discharged employees but refuse in whole or part to compensate for lost time by awarding back pay, they are in fact invoking the penalty of suspension for the period back pay is denied. In effect they are usually conceding the employer's right to lay off the employee for the period.

Suspension may be viewed as one of the most flexible of all penalties. It may be graduated in accordance with the seriousness of the offense: it may be for one hour, it may be for months. It may be about as mild as a slap on the wrist, or for so protracted a period that the employee is really invited to seek a job elsewhere. Since this disciplinary action lacks the finality of discharge, there is a good chance that in quite a few cases the action will not be challenged by the employee or the union.

(c) Demotion or Downgrading

The propriety of demotion or downgrading as a tool of discipline has perplexed arbitrators. When may an employer discipline his employee by demotion and be sustained by a reviewing arbitrator? Does the collective-bargaining agreement contemplate demotion as a disciplinary device? The agreement may exclude demotion either because of its effect upon the seniority rights of lower rated employees, or because it may be viewed as essentially unwise. If the agreement does not forbid the use of demotion, is demotion proper in the case in question?

[27] By permission from *Personnel Administration*, by Pigors & Myers. Copyright, 1947, McGraw-Hill Book Company, Inc. (at page 202).

In general, arbitrators subscribe to the thought that the penalty should fit the crime, and should be efficacious. Demotion for inefficiency is frequently directly related to the offense and may be sustained (particularly if there is promise that the employee will be able and willing to perform in a lower category). Demotion for dishonesty, insubordination, or other personality difficulties is apparently unrelated to the offense, and hardly remedial. Decisions of arbitrators tend to take considerations like these into account.

In so doing, the decisions reflect current thinking. One authority, commenting upon the doubtful wisdom of demotion as a disciplinary device, has stated:

> Demotions are . . . a questionable form of disciplinary action, except when there is a failure to meet established job standards. Demotion or downgrading to a former less skilled job is appropriate when a man has clearly failed to make good in a job to which he has temporarily been tried out. But once the trial period has passed and the employee continues on the higher rated job, the wisdom of subsequent demotion for poor performance is open to question. If the employee fails to improve after adequate warnings and constructive criticism, discharge may be a preferable action in order to avoid leaving permanently dissatisfied employees in the organization. As in nearly all cases of disciplinary action, however, discharge should be the last resort.[28]

(D) Transfer

In general, the same considerations may bear upon the right of a company to transfer out of his unit an employee for disciplinary reasons, where the transfer is not, strictly speaking, a demotion, but nevertheless results in loss of status such as unit seniority. Of course the employer may have retained unlimited power to transfer an employee. But where transfer with loss of status is subject to arbitral review, the arbitrator may want to be convinced that the action is appropriate and remedial. In a Ford Motor Company dispute, Harry Shulman observed.

> It is not necessary to pass here upon the broad question of whether a disciplinary penalty may ever take the form of a trans-

[28] *Id.*

fer from one job or seniority unit to another . . . a transfer seems to be quite inappropriate to the kind of an offense here involved. There is no relation between the nature of the offense and the nature of the job. It cannot be said that the offense here is of such a character as to render the employee unfit for the particular job while leaving him suitable for a different job to which he is transferred.[29]

On the other hand, transfer within a classification without loss of status may, when wisely used, be one of the most efficacious tools of management in preventing or removing disciplinary troubles. For example, where an employee cannot get along with his foreman because their personalities clash, it would be best, for the sake of everyone's blood pressure, to put him under some other foreman; if necessary, to give him another job in the same classification.

The solution to many problems of industrial discipline may lie in finding proper work assignments. Collective-bargaining agreements should permit management a large amount of freedom in this respect. Arbitrators (as they have sometimes done) should approve, as a remedial measure, transfer without demotion, (provided no loss of seniority or undue interference with the rights of other employees is involved), wherever it appears that a change of environment may be beneficial.

(E) Loss of Seniority

There are occasional instances in arbitration reports of the imposition by companies or arbitrators of the penalty of reduction of seniority status. (The penalty is, of course, frequently used in military discipline.) For example, one arbitrator imposed it in the case of a long-service employee who, in the arbitrator's opinion, should not have been discharged for insubordination but should not be permitted, by unqualified reinstatement, to get off scot-free. The penalty seems to have possibilities as a disciplinary measure particularly applicable to long-term employees, where discharge or

[29] Opinion A-34, 1943, Shulman and Chamberlain—Cases on Labor Relations, *supra*, p. 547.

other drastic penalty is considered inappropriate because of previous service with good record.

(F) Withholding of Monetary Benefits

Can a company withhold vacation pay as a penalty for absenteeism? In one case the arbitrator, in denying the right of the company, declared:

> Vacations should be regarded as an earned right rather than a gratuity given or withheld for punitive purposes. . . . It would seem that the remedy of the Company in the case of absenteeism is to determine the reason therefor and, if deemed unjustifiable, to discharge the employee. It is at that point that the Company would have the opportunity to negotiate with the Union regarding what constitutes "justifiable" reasons for absenteeism. Further, the Arbiter can find nothing in the Agreement which gives the Company the right to issue interpretative regulations regarding the employees' benefits as established under the Agreement.[30]

Vacation benefits are a part of the worker's wages. Withholding of vacation benefits is a kind of fine. Fines as such have practically disappeared with collective bargaining and established wage rates. An offending worker may be penalized by discharge or layoff; but he should not usually, by a fine, be made to work for less than the stipulated rate. To make him do so would, in general, seem to be contrary to the collective-bargaining agreement, at least in cases where the result is a cost-saving to the company.

There are, of course, exceptions. It might be permissible to dock an employee for damage to tools where the damage was negligently or wilfully caused. The responsibility of an employee for his own misconduct would be justification. And an arbitrator may sometimes suspend wage-benefit provisions as a penalty appropriate to the offense. In a Full Fashioned Hosiery Workers dispute, arbitrator G. Allen Dash, Jr., penalized workers for an illegal work stoppage by directing them to make up the time lost by working overtime on a straight-time pay basis. Under the circumstances, the "punishment" seemed to fit the "crime."

[30] Fearing, in Liberty Plating Co., 9 LA 505, 508 (1947).

The above are merely some of the ways in which management may exercise its disciplinary prerogative. There are many others—some of them subtler—refusal of promotion or merit increase, for example. Management would be well advised to become familiar with them all, for the proper use of each may be the best remedy for a specific problem. They must be used with finesse, with attention paid to the appropriateness of the penalty in view of the offense committed. Just as a surgeon must know his surgical instruments, just as a lawyer must know his forms of action, so management must know the kinds of penalties at its disposal.

Specific Instances of the Effect of Arbitration Upon Industrial Discipline

So far the general relation of the arbitration process to industrial discipline has been treated. The reader is now requested to make a ninety-degree turn from the cross-sectional to the vertical approach, from the conceptual to the functional. Let us turn our attention to specific kinds of situations where management may assert its power to discipline, and consider how the arbitration process has affected these situations. Utility lies more frequently in the specific than in the general. The inquiry will lead, first, to a consideration of the media through which management may express its disciplinary power, and second, to a consideration of some of the industrial offenses which are typically the ground for penal or corrective action.

First, with regard to the media or agencies of company policy: the written expression of company policy (the company rule) and the human agency of company policy (the foreman, the immediate supervisor). It is at the level of the company rule and the foreman that most workers make their day-to-day contact with company policy. If disciplinary measures of management, conceived at the high-echelon level of the polished conference table, are to be satisfactorily translated to those whom they affect, it behooves management to give care to the way in which those decisions are transmitted and received at the operating level.

(A) Company Rules

Company rules may be established by management for the purpose of governing the conduct of employees in many different ways. They may include safety rules, describing the precautions employees are required to take to minimize the risk of industrial accident (use of safety devices, smoking prohibited, etc.). They may include rules relating to the personal conduct of employees on the premises (no fighting, gambling, etc.). They may be more ambitious, and define broadly or particularly the several offenses, on and off the premises, which will render an employee subject to disciplinary action (insubordination, inefficiency, disloyalty, etc.). In other words, they may run the gamut from the particular to the general. Company rules may also state management policy on the nature of the penalty to be imposed for specific offenses ("price lists").

From a gleaning of arbitration reports, one may derive asserted principles of good practice with regard to company rules. These principles of good practice are premised upon certain propositions apparently rather generally recognized by arbitrators: First, management has not only the *right* to make unilateral pronouncements of working rules reasonably designed to implement its power to direct the working forces; it may in many instances have the *duty* as well, so that employees may be advised and take heed. (That is not to say that company rules are not the proper subject of collective bargaining.) Second, company rules which define the penalty can do no more than express the policy of the party who declares them; they cannot, without the authority of agreement, preclude the union from contesting the penalty in a specific grievance; they cannot predetermine the decision of the arbitrator.

It would be foolish to claim that one could prepare a reliable handbook of good practice in company rules from a reading of arbitration reports. Things are not that certain in arbitration. Arbitrators are too individualistic for that. But it is not surprising to come across decisions where arbitrators have declared that a company rule must be clear and unambiguous if it is to deal effectively with a previously doubtful situation and make violators properly subject to discipline. And that it must be proclaimed and published in a way that affords assurance that employees know and understand it. Private company rules, like secret traps, may not appeal to an arbitrator. The surprising thing is that these rather obvious points frequently recognized by arbitrators have sometimes been overlooked by management, and that arbitrators have occasion to apply them. Inefficiency of management in expressing company rules cannot contribute to good industrial relations.

Instances are encountered of arbitrations involving a rule-that-is-not-a-rule: the case of the company rule that is haphazardly enforced or not enforced by management. Company rules that deal with relatively trivial offenses are sometimes inconsistently applied. Disciplinary action in such cases may be widely resented by the workers, and engender suspicion that the disciplined offender is the object of discrimination. Obvious disparity of treatment may not be acceptable to the arbitrator. Of course a company can change its policy from lax enforcement to strict enforcement. It may conduct campaigns to secure observance. But this change of policy, if it is to appeal to some arbitrators, must be made known to employees in advance. To introduce the change in policy by "making an example" of one employee may not seem fair.

In their desire to be neat and orderly, and possibly fair and just, some companies have made a fetish of "consistency." They may promulgate a "price list"—a schedule of penalties to be applied without fear or favor upon the commission of stated offenses. If life were as simple and orderly as some of these price lists profess to be! But let the company put a rigid rule into effect as strictly as the pronouncement declares. It may be crucified for its "consistency," guilty, ironically, of ultimate inconsistency because it has treated as like fundamentally unlike cases. For consistency cannot always be literal. How the actual situations will arise to mock the superficial rule-maker! Provokingly they will not always fit nicely into the patterns that he has smugly delineated, into his little preconceived "rules and regulations." Even our criminal laws leave the precise penalty for the most part to the discretion of the judge.

This is not to deny that there may be advantages in price lists, to guard against indefensible differences in treatment for the same offense. But expert draftsmanship is required to make them as flexible as the actualities with which they deal.

Naturally, many arbitrators are not willing to concede that by the unilateral action of setting a schedule of penalties the company can take the question of the propriety of a specific application from the province of the arbitrator. But custom counts, and if for a long period of time a union tolerates the operation of a schedule of penalties, an arbitrator may find that it had acquiesced. If the union dislikes the schedule, it may be prudent to take the bull by the horns, make the schedule a grievance, or negotiate.

Where the price list is incorporated into the collective-bargaining agreement, the arbitrator's penalty-review power may be curtailed. One authority, considering such a frozen schedule of penalties, declared:

> Such a treatment of the discipline problem completely departs from the theory that disciplinary measures are taken for the sole purpose of preventing breaches of discipline. Mere mechanical imposition of penalties prevents the consideration of each case on its own merits, with appropriate consideration to the background, the causes, the likelihood of repetition, the attitude of the employee, the effect on the department, etc. So much necessarily depends on the employee's attitude and record, so much can be done by constructive measures including counseling, transfer, temporary demotion, adjustment of family problems, etc., that a list of penalties for each breach of discipline is a superficial approach to the problem. Moreover, no contract can contain a complete list of all possible violations of discipline, nor of appropriate measures to be taken to prevent their repetition.[31]

In the opinion of George W. Taylor, the use of price lists

[31] By permission from *Management at the Bargaining Table,* by Hill & Hook. Copyright, 1945, McGraw-Hill Book Company, Inc. (At page 103.)

to circumvent individual grievance settlement is inadvisable:

> There are incomparable values in collective bargaining conceived as a gradual emergence of mutual understanding through grievance settlements. This is apparent as respects discipline. Discipline is a delicate tool of management, most useful when applied with regard for plant necessities and employee equities in particular cases. The kind and degree of discipline appropriate in certain situations cannot be forecast. There can be, therefore, no sound by-passing of the grievance settlement process by a long listing of employee offenses and applicable penalties in the labor contract. In my opinion, discipline cannot be formalized by making up such a price list and continue to serve as an effective tool of management. In other words, much of the collective bargaining that is implicit in grievance settling can't be avoided by making the labor agreement more explicit. . . .[32]

In general, arbitration awards demonstrate that propriety of a company rule is an arbitrable question if it affects the conditions of employment. The company should know that an unreasonable company rule is not sacrosanct because it is called a rule; that violation of a company rule is not inevitably "just cause" for discipline. Employees and unions have the right to object to such rules as contrary to the collective-bargaining agreement. On the other hand, the union and all employees should know that defiance of a company rule on the ground that it is unreasonable or illegal is perilous; insubordination is not the answer. The prescribed way of contesting the validity of a company rule is by use of the grievance procedure.

(B) Foremen

The coming of age of collective bargaining and the arbitration process has also had its effect upon the disciplinary powers of foremen—the human agency of company authority. The foreman is to a factory what the committeeman is to a party, or what the sergeant is to the army. It is chiefly through him that workers see management. Good industrial relations depend upon good foremen.

There was a time when it was frequent practice to delegate

32 26 Personnel, 232, 237. (American Management Association, Inc.)

to foremen absolute disciplinary powers, including the right to discharge on the spot. There was no doubt then about their prestige. But the abuses to which such system was subject were inherent in its decentralization. There would be little uniformity of discipline practices throughout the plant. There would be tough foremen and easy-going foremen. There would be careful foremen and rash foremen. Some of them might act harshly without proper examination of the facts.

The protections to workers afforded by the grievance machinery and arbitration compel a reëxamination of the role of the foreman as an enforcer of discipline policy. The necessity of defending its actions in response to a grievance may persuade management to channel serious discipline cases for higher review by the line or staff before final action is taken. The evidence must be checked. Penalties must be reasonable and reflect general company practice.

Such powers as are frequently left to foremen are the lesser powers of verbal warning and reporting offenses (with recommendations) for action by higher authority. Of course the practice is not standardized, and instances may be found of foremen still having more drastic powers, such as the power to suspend on the spot, or even to discharge. But a company may run into trouble in arbitration if it has the responsibility of defending a foreman's drastic action without having sufficient control over it. And reversal of a foreman's action at one of the steps in the grievance procedure may impair his prestige much more than depriving him of final authority.

The carefulness now required of companies in handling their discipline problems highlights the importance of properly selected and trained foremen. More attention is being given to the psychological attributes of a good foreman. Management must also be sure that its foremen are properly instructed, so that they may be able to prevent disciplinary problems, or know precisely what to do if the occasion for discipline arises. If management fails in this respect, it has only itself to blame. For example.

It is the function of the company to inform its foremen fully as to their rights, authorities, and duties. The foreman evidently felt that the circumstances were such that he would have preferred to give the "white slip" alone and not to impose the lay-off had he known he had authority to do so. The company's failure to instruct and train its foreman fully, therefore, led to the mistake which resulted in the two days' lay-off.[33]

When a foreman has drastic disciplinary powers, and apparently makes a mistake, he puts management on the spot. To reverse him may weaken his prestige in the eyes of his men. Sometimes management may believe it best to bluff the thing through, to contest the ensuing grievance (even though contest is hopeless) as a measure of face-saving, in line with its policy of backing up its supervisors. It will share the responsibility for the mistake. But an arbitrator may not be impressed:

The company has raised the point that it is opposed to the reinstatement of Eggleston because it would reflect unfavorably on Adams, whom they wish to retain as a supervisor, and might possibly create a morale or discipline problem in the department. The arbitrator is cognizant of the difficulties involved in maintaining proper discipline, but he does not agree that the way to secure respect for a foreman is to back him up in his decisions whether they are right or wrong. The object of industrial discipline is future improvement and not retribution or "saving face" for the foreman.[34]

On the other hand, management may put the foreman on the spot. Frequently the conscientious foreman must feel let down by management when he has taken a position on certain objectionable conduct of a worker, only to have management reverse him for reasons of strategy or expediency. There must also be many times when the foreman in taking a seemingly arbitrary position is merely carrying out management's explicit instructions. He may be forced to bear the brunt of unpopularity through no fault of his own. The foreman is often the whipping-boy of industrial relations.

[33] Updegraff, in Standard Oil Co. of Indiana, 11 LA 689, 691 (1948).

[34] Prasow, in International Minerals & Chemical Corp., 4 LA 127, 130 (1946).

(c) INEFFICIENCY

Management, acting through its supervisors and directives, is still concerned with the same age-old types of disciplinary problems. Their face may change as times change, but their identity is the same: inefficiency, insubordination, dishonesty, etc. They are the names used when an employer charges that a worker is not giving what was bargained.

The policies which management will apply in coping with the problems behind these names must be affected by its own needs and powers. The worldly wise counsels of supply and demand—opportunism—may be heeded. Management may try to get as much for its money as possible. When labor is readily available, it may impose high standards of performance; the converse, when labor is scarce. It may lack free will: the great god Competition may pull the strings.

The manpower needs of today call upon management to reappraise its employment policies (including discipline) to the end that the highest practical number of people may be used. In particular, management must now employ and retain workers who in other times would be deemed too inefficient for profitable use. This being the case, every avenue must be explored to raise the efficiency level of marginal and submarginal producers.

In the quest for efficiency of production, management needs to make no apology. No express provision in a collective-bargaining agreement is required to articulate the power of the employer to discipline and discharge for fundamental breach of contract. Every employee upon acceptance of employment promises to do a fair day's work. Of course that is not easy to define. In the nature of things, and under any economic system, management may not be able to tolerate real inefficiency. Like a corrosive it may slow down production, wear out machines, waste materials, duplicate effort, and possibly result in the unemployment of the efficient. In a competitive situation, it may take the profit out of the venture and close the plant. Even in the tightest times, the basically inefficient, the unsalvageable, are unemployable.

Only an unwise arbitrator would not concede to management the basic right to remove the forever inefficient workers, if that were all there was to the case. But that may not be all. The pot should not call the kettle black. The inefficiency of the employee may be really the inefficiency of the employer. It may be a symptom only, or a secondary infection, the primary infection being elsewhere. Arbitrators want to know these things, for he who comes into equity must do equity.

The knowledge that arbitrators will be interested in the background of alleged inefficiency should prod management to be sure that none of the causes of a worker's inefficiency is its own responsibility. One company, for example, made the mistake of dismissing a weaver who had fallen down on the job after the company had failed to supply swords and replacement parts for its looms. The arbitrator declared:

> I do not question the right of the Company to discipline, discharge, and transfer to another job, an employee who is unable to do efficient work. . . . I think, however, that as a prerequisite to taking such action, the Company is under a duty to have its machinery and equipment in reasonably good condition so that the employees have a fair chance. It is true that the efficiency of those two employees was lower than that of the room generally, but bad conditions will affect different people differently. Phlegmatic people are able to take things in stride, while those of a nervous disposition may be very much upset. Mrs. Mount has been a good weaver for too long a time to deserve being taken off the job without a fair opportunity to show that she is still a good weaver if given reasonably good looms to work on.[35]

Arbitrations over discipline for inefficiency are replete with inquiries such as: Was an employee's inefficiency attributable to assignment of excessive work? Was the employer in good faith in assigning the employee to a particular job? Was an employee's alleged carelessness or inefficiency due to inexperience, or inadequate instruction, inspection, or supervision? Was the real cause of an accident faulty equipment? Was an employee's failure to meet production standards the result of too rapid upgrading? Should an employee

[35] McCoy, in Dwight Mfg. Co., 10 LA 786, 790 (1948).

have been transferred (or downgraded) instead of discharged?

The interest of arbitrators in such matters may be for some companies a blessing in disguise. In the airing of the grievance, they have the opportunity to hear their workers express candid (and sometimes caustic) opinions on plant operations. These opinions may be biased, but they come from first-hand knowledge. If management is not oversensitive, if it has a keen appreciation of the fact that no system of operations has ever been devised which cannot stand some improvement, much may be salvaged even from a lost cause in terms of the larger values that come from self-examination and corrective action. The hearing may bring forth, the arbitrator may point out, faults that are discreetly unmentioned by supervisors because most people just want to mind their own business, and shy away from making criticisms that may give offense. Management is ill advised if it is too proud to listen to lesser people or outsiders.

In the sloughing off of the inefficient, arbitrators may challenge management to the exercise of due care and forbearance. An arbitrator's sympathy goes especially to the worker who seems to be making a sincere effort. Possibly management is asking too much: possibly its production standards are at fault. Is there no place in the plant for a sincere worker? Suppose he is inefficient—if he is really trying, there may be hope for him. Slow learners may some day learn well.

The particularly hard case is that of the worker past his prime, who has been for long a faithful and efficient employee, but who is now suffering from the creeping inefficiency of old age. Should management be permitted to discharge him? Here is a case which may twang the heartstrings. (Would a blanket retirement policy be better?) One arbitrator reluctantly sustained the removal of aged workers from their job, but refused to approve an outright discharge:

It would be going against the entire intent and spirit of seniority clauses in general and this clause in particular, were we to hold that the failure of long-term employees ultimately, because of age, to meet production standards is a proper cause for discharge. It must be remembered that seniority is plant-wide in this establishment. There may be some job that those people will be able to do if there should be an increase in production activity in this plant in the future.[36]

Of course, not every collective-bargaining agreement may give the arbitrator such latitude.

The indefiniteness of much of the proof, the frequency of cases that are not clear cut, the usual apparent good faith of the grievant, make arbitrations for inefficiency among the most difficult in the field of discipline problems. It seems to require a strong case to uphold drastic action like discharge in the case of a long-service employee.

(D) INSUBORDINATION

Inefficiency is frequently based on lack of ability or unintentional neglect. A different type of offense—raising different problems—is based on wilful misconduct. In such category fall the various kinds of disobedience. An employee may subject himself to discipline by separate action, such as insubordination including refusal to perform assigned work, or by participation in wrongful group activities, such as illegal work stoppages, strikes, and slowdowns. Sometimes there is no other name for it but pure recalcitrance.

The undiluted case can hardly awaken the sympathies of the arbitrator. There is little room in industry for the back-seat driver who tries to get control of the steering wheel. There are still some workers and unions who need to know that they should not break contracts and take the law into their own hands, that they have no right to dictate how a plant is to be run. Orders must be obeyed. If they think management is wrong, the remedy is not disobedience, but resort, as promised, to the grievance procedure.

The grievance procedure is prescribed in the contract precisely because the parties anticipated that there would be claims of violations which would require adjustment. That procedure is prescribed for all grievances, not merely for doubtful ones. Noth-

36 Brandschain, in Dodge Cork Co., Inc., 8 LA 250, 253 (1947).

ing in the contract even suggests the idea that only doubtful violations need be processed through the grievance procedure and that clear violations can be resisted through individual selfhelp. The only difference between a "clear" violation and a doubtful one is that the former makes a clear grievance and the latter a doubtful one.

. . . an industrial plant is not a debating society. Its object is production. When a controversy arises, production cannot wait for exhaustion of the grievance procedure. While that procedure is being pursued, production must go on. And some one must have the authority to direct the manner in which it is to go on until the controversy is settled. That authority is vested there because the responsibility for production is vested there; and responsibility must be accompanied by authority.[37]

In the words of another arbitrator:

. . . acceptance of the authority of the company and its agents . . . is a basic necessity in any enterprise. If management were obligated to beg or persuade employees to carry out reasonable orders each time they were given, the enterprise simply could not operate efficiently. Management must retain the right to direct the working forces, and efficient direction requires the maintenance of discipline. As has often been pointed out, the maintenance of discipline involves delicate personal relationships. One in authority must meet every challenge to that authority with firmness. Any resort to debate or quibbling is likely to be interpreted as a sign of weakness or uncertainty.

This is a basic problem in collective bargaining. The essence of the problem is how to give management adequate power to perform its vital functions and yet to prevent tyrannical abuses of that power. Collective agreements attempt to solve this problem by giving management the right to direct the working forces while reserving to the employee the right to appeal any alleged abuses to the grievance machinery.[38]

But there are limits to obedience. Management should appreciate that its order-giving power is not absolute. An order can be so unreasonable, so clearly invalid, that an employee cannot be disciplined for refusal to obey. For example, the assignment of skilled workers to jobs outside their classification may be completely beyond the power of manage-

[37] Shulman, in Ford Motor Co., 3 LA 779, 781 (1944).

[38] Killingsworth, in Triumph Explosives, Inc., 2 LA 617, 618 (1945).

ment. In a Ford Motor Company dispute, Arbitrator Harry Shulman reinstated a group of glaziers who had refused to accept work as painters when there was no glazing work available. He found that nothing in the contract empowered the company to transfer or lend skilled workers from one classification to another:

> . . . Admittedly the painting work was not part of the glazier's classification and was in no way related to it. Nor was there any emergency or unusual reason for the assignment. It is a bald case in which a skilled tradesman was assigned to work wholly different from and unrelated to his classification because of a shortage of work in his own classification or a desire to get the other work done . . .
> Nothing in Opinion A-116 (3 LA 779) justifies the disciplinary action in this case. That opinion dealt primarily with production employees. It may be applied to the skilled classifications in situations where there is reasonable dispute as to whether the work assigned does or does not fall within the employee's classification. . . . But it cannot be extended to assignments of work in admittedly different skilled trades constituting different seniority groups. The company does not have the same right of transferring . . . skilled tradesmen from one classification to another that it has with respect to employees in production classifications.[39]

In another case, a company disciplined an employee who had refused to work in inclement weather after he had been working under heated conditions indoors. The arbitrators, in reversing the company's action, observed, "Resort to grievance procedure is not an antidote for pneumonia."[40]

The fact that an employee has been insubordinate or refused to work does not always shock the arbitrator so much that he will sustain the severest discipline without further ado. Here, as in other cases, management may find itself defending as well as attacking. What was it that caused the employee thus to flout authority? Was he goaded into insubordination by provocation? Or, taking another view, did he really flout authority, or simply not understand?

Sometimes management attempts to teach an employee a

[39] Shulman, in Ford Motor Co., 3 LA 782 (1946).
[40] Elson, in Hegeler Zinc Co., 8 LA 826 (1947).

lesson in obedience and ends by receiving from the arbitrator a lesson in personnel administration. Consider, for example, the following language from an arbitrator's opinion:

> . . . he could only be guilty of insubordination if he understood that he was being ordered and if so understanding his answer constituted a refusal and not a statement of what he preferred to do. I do not mean that it was improper to put the order in the form of a question. That is probably as good a way as any to give one nor do I mean that the dispatcher should have repeated it, or insisted, threatened, or tried to persuade. What I do think should have been done was to have let that man know that his response to the question was being considered as a refusal to obey an order. Even in the Army where unfaltering obedience is required and necessary, it is customary, in the few instances, where an order is not given originally and in an unmistakable tone, to say "That's an order" or words of similar import so that there can be no mistake about it, before initiating disciplinary action.
> Here there was such a complete mood of nonchalance or indifference about the entire matter that the man might well have felt that he was being excused. Without having had resort to bickering, argument, cajolery or repetition, devices which supervisors are clearly not required to make use of, it still seems to me that the man should have been let known that there was a finality and decisiveness about the matter and that his answer if unchanged would have consequences more serious than appeared from the manner with which the situation was treated at that time.[41]

Similarly, management should be careful to distinguish between a real refusal to work and a failure to carry out orders for lack of time or other valid reasons. And since companies that prevent most please arbitrators most, management should see that all workers clearly know their duties and responsibilities, so that misunderstanding does not result in a hot-headed refusal to work.

More serious problems for the arbitrator are presented when he reviews disciplinary action taken to deal with illegal group activities, such as strikes. If ever arbitrators were tried and tested, it is here.

We are concerned at this point not with lawful strikers, but with the illegal variety. The illegality of a strike may be made

[41] Burke, in Dairymen's League Cooperative Assn., 11 LA 1113, 1114 (1948).

clear by the fact that it is in violation of a no-strike clause in the collective-bargaining agreement. Not that an express no-strike clause is necessary to make a particular strike illegal. Most collective-bargaining agreements contain implied obligations not to strike. But still an express no-strike clause is useful. It may give possibilities of legal action under the Taft-Hartley Act. It may be worded broadly enough to make it clear that a real or fancied breach of contract by the employer will not, on a tit-for-tat basis, release union and workers from their obligation not to strike, their obligation to resort to the grievance procedure. Properly drawn, the no-strike clause may go a long way in minimizing the significance to an arbitrator of mistakes the company may have made in matters leading up to the strike. Even so, manifestation of continued willingness to bargain collectively, good faith coöperation in making the grievance machinery work, will be expected of the employer. He cannot sabotage the peaceful means of settling disputes by endless delays, hair-splitting tactics, etc., and then throw up holy hands in righteous protest over a union, which he has driven half-crazy, finally breaking the no-strike clause. In one particular case, the arbitrator held the company partly to blame for a strike by reason of its vacillation and "double talk" in negotiating grievances with union representatives. He observed: "While that is no justification for their strike action, it does affect the propriety and extent of the penalty to be imposed."[42]

All in all, when we find employees acting as a group in disregard of a no-strike pledge to which their union has committed them, we have in extreme form a breakdown in the spirit of harmony and mutuality which alone can give industrial peace and make a collective-bargaining relationship worth while. It is the kind of thing which calls for an inquest. Personnel directors and union officials, acting like coroners, should be interested in ascertaining all the circumstances which contributed to the illegal strike, to the end that correc-

[42] Whiting, in New York Car Wheel Co., 7 LA 183, 190 (1947).

tive measures may be taken. Arbitration hearings (based on resulting discipline grievances) sometimes furnish an excellent opportunity for inquest.

Let us consider one arbitrated dispute as a clinical study of the tangled web of circumstances that may culminate in an illegal strike.[43] On April 17, 1944, the pourers of the E. Foundry Company went on strike, in violation of a no-strike clause in the collective-bargaining agreement. As a result, the E. Company discharged six men as the alleged instigators of and leaders of the strike.

The arbitration revealed that behind this crisis in industrial relations there was a long history of unresolved conflict between the pourers and the company. Contention had developed over the rate and allocation of overtime work. For some time the pourers had felt abused over the fact that the company had been giving all overtime work in pouring to the molders, and offering the pourers instead spruing work for overtime. They charged that the Company was paying molders at time and one-half their molding rate for overtime work in pouring (a lower-rate job), but was unwilling to pay the pourers time and one-half their pouring rate for overtime spruing work (lower than the pouring rate). It was felt that the pourers were unfairly treated both with respect to the amount and the rate of overtime work offered them. The dispute simmered and boiled. There were twenty-three work stoppages. Finally, the strike.

If there had been a genuine interest on both sides in peaceful settlement, there were opportunities aplenty to iron out the difficulties in an equitable way before affairs reached fever pitch.

When the arbitrator analyzed events in retrospect, he concluded that both company and union had some measure of responsibility for the final outburst.

Chief causes of the strike, in the opinion of the arbitrator, were the fault of the union:

[43] Eberhard Mfg. Co., 4 LA 419 (1944). (Miller, Arbitrator.)

1. The union, including the members of the committee, its officers, and international representatives, had failed to properly and intelligently advise their members and the workers whom they represent as to their duties and obligations under the terms of the existing agreement.
2. All the union representatives failed to follow the grievance procedure established in the agreement to the same extent that they failed to take disciplinary action against members who wilfully and recurringly violated the no-strike pledge contained in the agreement. This failure to take proper disciplinary action undoubtedy convinced the workers that their repetitive work stoppages were more or less condoned by the union.
3. The failure of the union officers and committeemen to correctly interpret certain provisions of the agreement, especially with respect to the extra spruing work given the pourers and the extra-pouring work given the molders, unwarrantedly instilled in the minds of the workers a feeling that the company was retaliating in some manner or trying to arbitrarily impose an unfair basis of compensation for the extra work. The extra and after-regular-shift work could not be considered as a transfer to other work by the widest stretch of the imagination. It was essentially an opportunity, given the molders and pourers, to earn extra money by working extra hours at an entirely different type of work. To insist that these men be paid other than time and one-half the regular rate of the job was ridiculous to say the least.
4. The history of work stoppages amongst the pourers is proof sufficient that both A . . . and S . . . were irresponsible union committeemen . . . indicated beyond a shadow of a doubt that they delegated to themselves arrogant powers and a militant attitude which the pourers mistook for competent guidance. . . . Note: Employees election to office in a union or membership of a union committee does not immunize such employees from disciplinary action when their conduct warrants such action. As union officers or members of a union committee, they are supposed to follow procedure established in an agreement and, at the same time, set an example for others to follow.

But the company had some part in the final crisis:

7. The company, like the union, failed to require grievance procedures to be followed and by its dilatory tactics failed to take disciplinary action when the stoppages began to be quite numerous. On the other hand, the company did over-appease the pourers. Long ago, the company should have exercised its inher-

ent right of discharge when workers refused to work. There is little question but that lack of manpower was the chief reason for the company failing to take proper disciplinary action.[44]

While sustaining the discharges, the arbitrator found it appropriate to make certain recommendations to assist the company and union in preventing recurrence of industrial strife. These included proposals for allocation and rate of overtime work (a more equitable division of overtime work between molders and pourers than the company had in effect); establishment of orderly grievance procedure—including reduction of grievances to writing and prompt disposal of grievances; and further, that first, second, and third offenses be treated differently:

> Before discharge have two phases of punitive action. For the first infraction, give the employee a reprimand but notify the union committee. For the second infraction, give a disciplinary layoff but notify the union committee or preferably give the disciplinary layoff by joint action of the union committee and the company. For the third infraction, give a discharge, subject to the approval of the union committee. In all cases be sure of your facts.[45]

The above case is not an isolated instance. It frequently happens that both company and union share the ultimate responsibility for the complete breakdown in relations manifested by a strike. In an American Steel and Wire Company dispute, the Arbitration Board analyzed the situation as follows:

> From the evidence introduced on the record this board believes that the happenings with which the grievances are concerned signify an inadequacy on the part of both parties in observing the intent of proper collective bargaining. This board believes that, if each of the parties had approached the problem of instituting the 20-turn schedule in a more considerate mood, consonant with the spirit of good labor relations, the unfortunate results dealt within the grievances could have been avoided.[46]

But the participants, rather than the company, must fre-

[44] *Ibid.* at 424.
[45] *Ibid.* at 425.
[46] Blumer and Kelly in 5 LA 193, 212 (1946), Shulman and Chamberlain, *supra*, p. 481.

quently bear the larger responsibility for engaging in strikes or other means of group force, particularly where the collective-bargaining agreement expressly binds them not to resort to such means in protest over real or alleged grievances. Frequently such action on their part shows irresponsibility, a failure to appreciate that a labor contract works both ways—binds them as well as the company. In one case the umpire observed:

> While the matter was not considered at the hearing, it is public knowledge that the discharge of these three men led to a short stoppage of work at the Lincoln plant. I cannot refrain from expressing the regret and disappointment which this stoppage has caused me as it must have caused also the Union and the Company. This was the kind of thing which happened with too great frequency prior to the umpire agreement and during its early operation. But, in due course, the impropriety of such stoppages was generally recognized. It was recognized that, from all points of view, the grievance procedure is the civilized, economical, and established method for correcting alleged misapplications of the agreement—and most particularly in disciplinary cases. We all took pride in the Ford employees' later record of responsibility in this respect. This sudden relapse is therefore quite regrettable. Surely the stoppage was wholly pointless and wasteful. It caused loss of earnings to numerous innocent employees as well as the company. It subjected employees to disciplinary penalties for participation in the stoppage. It endangered the very case of the discharged employees. It struck a blow at the prestige and standing of the union. It threw an additional obstacle in the way of future collective bargaining and harmonious labor relations. And it did all this when a wholly adequate, civilized, and economical procedure was available to protect the interests involved without loss to anyone. Such reckless and wanton waste must be strenuously avoided.[47]

The arbitrator used this stern language in spite of the fact that he found that the discharge of the workers which precipitated the work stoppage had not been preceded by an adequate investigation and was hasty and ill-considered.

A problem that faces management, in dealing with illegal group activities, is the selection of offenders who should be

[47] Shulman, in Ford Motor Co., 6 LA 853, 854 (1946).

singled out for discipline. While theoretically all workers participating in a strike, work stoppage, or slow-down may be guilty of breach of contract and subject to disciplinary action, it may not be appropriate to treat them all alike. In the first place, mass discipline may hurt the company as much as the men. In the second place, it tends to defeat its purpose, since it unites, rather than divides, the men. In the third place, all men may not be equally guilty—an arbitrator may draw distinction between leaders and followers, between aggressive participants and those who are forced to go along. Management usually finds it desirable, therefore, to discipline on a selective basis—to take action against the ringleaders and let the followers off.

Selection of strike leaders is frequently difficult. It may be difficult to discover who were the leaders; it may be more difficult to prove to an arbitrator that they were the leaders. It is typical of management tactics to take action against union officials, on the premise that they bear the responsibility. The question that an arbitrator faces in such case is: To what extent will he require the company to prove actual leadership by union officials? Or to what extent will he presume leadership (or at least responsibility) because a man holds a union office? In other words, must the company show that the union officials were guilty of inciting to strike, or leading the men in strike activities, such as picketing? Or is it sufficient that it appears that the union officials participated in the strike? Or is it sufficient that the union officials did not do all in their power to advise the men against their illegal activity? We could hardly expect arbitrators to take a completely uniform position with regard to these questions.

In a discipline dispute growing out of a wildcat strike, the arbitrator had occasion to comment on the attitude of a union official:

One of the committeemen explained his credo as follows: he is opposed to wildcat, unauthorized strikes and would accordingly do all he could to dissuade employees from engaging in them; but if his advice goes unheeded and the employees form a picket line, his place is in the line with them. . . . This is a romantic expression of a perverse and debasing view of the committeeman's obligations. A committeeman is not merely a friend of the employees, tied to them by bonds of sympathy and loyalty. He is also a Union member and a Union official. He has taken his "obligation" to the Union; and, through the Union, he has pledged his honor and assumed the legal duty to observe the Contract with the Company. It is not a breach of his loyalty to his men to insist that they perform their duties . . . or to refuse to lead or join them in contrary conduct.[48]

It should be noted that the legality or propriety of disciplinary action for illegal group activities may be affected by the settlement agreement that management and union may enter into at the end of a strike, work stoppage or slow-down. If management intends to take disciplinary action against certain employees after a settlement has been reached, it should be careful to reserve its rights in this respect. Otherwise the workers may get a wrong impression, and more harm than good is done because of a suggestion of bad faith.

Another source of misunderstanding may arise, after the settlement of an illegal strike, through the failure of management to reinstate all participants in the strike. It has been recognized that management has the right and power, during the pendency of an illegal strike, to hire new workers to replace striking employees, and to retain these workers after the strike is ended, in preference to employees who have been replaced. Obviously the assertion of this power may engender a considerable amount of ill feeling and misunderstanding, and it would behoove management to make its position clear at the time of any settlement if it intends to exercise this power.

(e) Absence From Work

The arbitrator has also had some part to play in the development of procedures to combat absence offenses, such as absenteeism (excessive absence) and absence without leave. Arbitrators have recognized the importance of the problem:

[48] Shulman, in Ford Motor Co., Opinion A-150 (1944), Shulman and Chamberlain, supra, page 432.

No mill can operate successfully without regular attendance of the employees. Irregular attendance, by cutting down on profitable operations, hurts not only the company but the employees as well. Wages are paid out of profits. The employee who by his or her actions interferes with profitable operation creates a situation which not only prevents increases of wages for the other employees but actually jeopardizes their jobs.[49]

The question that confronts management, in dealing with the grave problem of absenteeism, is what disciplinary measures, including discharge, fit within the framework of "just cause," and are likely to be upheld by an arbitrator?

The difficulty in any other approach to absenteeism has led some employers to take drastic action against employees who have a numerical record of absence excessive as compared with plant average or some other standard, without going into the facts-behind-the-facts, the merits of each case. When disciplinary policy fails to take into account the equities, in the minds of some arbitrators at least, it may be too rough to be just:

. . . discipline may be amply justified in instances of excessive absences. The determination of the propriety for and the reasonableness of the penalty must take into account such factors as seniority, previous warnings directed to improvement in attendance records; the number of absences complained of; the alleged reasons for the absences, and whether or not the employees reported off.[50]

The clinical approach of many arbitrators may be manifested by interest in mitigating factors. Their attitude toward a grievance may be colored by a miscellany of factors—to take an example, the employee's transportation problems. If absenteeism or lateness is due to lack of dependable transportation to and from work, the arbitrator may feel that the remedy is not to discharge the employee, but to require him to make better arrangements.

Similar problems beset the employer in his attempt to deal with unexcused absence. He may find the arbitrator unsympathetic to a discharge of an employee for a first offense of

[49] McCoy, in Goodyear Clearwater Mills, 5 LA 619, 620 (1946).
[50] Gilden, in John Morrell and Company, 9 LA 931, 935 (1948).

this kind. Moreover, he will probably find that his own practices may come up for inspection. An unreasonable company rule may precipitate an absence without leave. A rule that under *no* circumstances will leave be granted during the Christmas period may be too simple to be realistic, and a case may arise where an employee has a right to a leave, despite the rule. An abrupt change of mind by management, which has the effect, with little advance notice and no explanation, of depriving employees of an expected day off, or an unanticipated rejection at the last moment of an employee's request for a particular vacation period, may constitute unreasonable conduct on the part of management and go to mitigate the offense committed by employees in being absent without leave.

On the other hand, unions and employees also have things to learn from the arbitration of absence cases. There are numerous instances of the tendency of unions to beat dead horses, to condone the inexcusable, to plead for an employee who does not deserve their support. There are, for example, cases in which the excuse of "illness" is of the flimsiest construction. Unions are only injuring themselves when they seem to support a flagrant disregard of the duty of regular attendance. Sometimes they may get away with it—reading reports of arbitrations on absenteeism and related offenses, one cannot but suspect that in some cases the union and the grievant were able to pull the wool over the arbitrator's eyes. Sometimes there is little the arbitrator can do—the man had a doctor's certificate, didn't he? (Even though he acted like a well man when off work.)

A mistake unions sometimes make is coming to the defense of employees whose attendance record is so poor that, regardless of the cause of absence, they have demonstrated a complete inutility. The presence of deadwood, the lazy, the chronically ill—whatever it is that accounts for an intolerable attendance record—breaks down production, prevents the proper division of labor, leads to unemployment of others. What can a union really hope to gain by challenging the discharge of an employee who, in a seven-month period following the union's agreement that she would have to improve her attendance record and prove herself physically able to work, had worked only slightly more than one-half of the scheduled working hours? There is the type that may be called the habitual offender:

> This total number of absent hours was far in excess of the plant average. Sometimes he would leave early in the day, but more often he would arrive late for work or not arrive at all. Sometimes his absences were excused, but more often they were not. All too frequently he would be absent for days at a time. And all too frequently his absences would occur after paydays and before or after weekends, thus warranting legitimate suspicion of outside interests and influences contributing to his inefficiency. On one occasion in February, 1947, he was suspended for one week for being intoxicated at night on company premises.[51]

A man may work so intermittently that he is really just a part-timer. Even illness can be overdone as an excuse. In one case, the arbitrator interpreted a provision granting leaves of absence for illness as follows:

> Intermittent absenteeism amounting to part-time employment is an entirely different situation. Here, the effects are felt by both the Company and the employees. Production decreases, with a subsequent effect on wages. Bottlenecks occur, resulting in otherwise unnecessary overtime, the necessity of shifting jobs and an inability to offer or receive regular work.
>
> Absenteeism caused by illness can be divided into two categories. First, there is the illness or injury which requires a relatively fixed period or periods of absence. A worker's position is not placed in jeopardy due to provisions such as Section 13. Second, there is the illness or injury or physical disability necessitating one or two absences per week. This prevents an employee from meeting his obligations to the Company and to his fellow employees. Regardless of the reason for such absences, lacking a contract provision requiring the Company to retain part-time employees, or physically handicapped employees, under Section 3 the Company may be justified in discharging such employees for failure to reasonably comply with the five day week as established by Section 7(a).[52]

[51] Dow Chemical Co., 12 LA 1070, 1071 (1949).

[52] Soule, in Rock Hill Printing & Finishing Co., 14 LA 153, 155 (1949).

In Conclusion

In the arbitration of discipline problems, both company and union buy the benefits of experience. During the drama of the arbitration hearing, the real dispute between the parties sometimes makes its appearance for the first time. In the presence of the arbitrator they have the opportunity to see themselves as others see them. It may not always be a pretty sight; the countenance may not be such as to attract unstinted admiration. If they rise the morrow morn sadder and wiser, the parties may have gained in typical human fashion a more mature viewpoint.

Through the arbitration process, employers and unions have been, and are being, forced to recast their policies and practices in the administration of discipline. The parties may not view the results as ideal. Employers have learned that it may be inadvisable to take drastic action against an employee if they do not feel confident that such action will stick upon appeal, or at least that management can give a good account of itself.

Against the disadvantage of having to submit disciplinary action for review by arbitration, may be set off advantages which enlightened management may come to recognize. When arbitrators throw the spotlight upon the employer's practices, the inquiry may be unpleasant but salutary. It may lead to corrective action. The effect may be like fresh air in a musty room. For despite all, there continue to be many instances where the evidence reveals that management has been guilty of poor tactics and bad practice in its disciplinary action.

Aside from the fact that arbitration is in any event almost always preferable to a strike, enlightened management may come to appreciate that from its viewpoint possibly the greatest advantage in submitting disciplinary problems to arbitration may be that, by such sacrifice of prerogative, its employees will acquire a greater sense of job security. Rightly or wrongly, most employees, including the good and efficient, fear arbitrary action. The knowledge that they are protected from such action, however unfounded the fear of it may be, will improve their morale and contribute to increased efficiency. Their sense of security may persuade them to remain with the job and do it well.

In those cases where management succeeds in vindicating its position before the arbitrator, its prestige is increased. Management has demonstrated its fairness, and shown the more reasonable employees that their union is not always right. (Of course there may be charges that the arbitrator was incompetent or dishonest.) Such things as groundless claims that discrimination was practiced against an employee because of his union activity may be exploded.

Similar benefits may be derived by workers and unions from the arbitration process. Unions and their members have the opportunity to acquire the virtue of being reasonable, as they mature in their attitude toward collective bargaining. They too have learned that arbitration is not a one-way street. They have also learned that the process does not always bring ideal results. They cannot always prove what they suspect. Idle allegations of malice, bird-dogging, discrimination may collapse, and they may feel that the employer can still get away with a great deal.

But all in all, the arbitration process offers unions and workers more advantages than disadvantages. What real substitute is there? Arbitration is the only substitute for strike or suit in court. The strike is too heavy and costly a bludgeon for most discipline cases. Court suits for damages can hardly be the answer. Thus the rights of individual workers are effectively protected by arbitration, whereas without arbitration they would be quite vulnerable. By protecting each worker, all workers are protected. Without such protection, there would be little meaning to the collective-bargaining agreement. The power of the arbitrator to reinstate is one of the great fundamentals of modern industrial relations.

Even in cases where the union loses its case, its purpose may be satisfied. There are doubtless times when the union does not believe in the merits of the grievance, but is forced by internal political considerations to represent the grievant. But the union may learn, after the expenditure of time and money, that groundless grievances do not in the long run pay. Even if they win cases which they should not win, they may inflame management and make it recalcitrant.

Enlightened unions, like enlightened management, may also derive benefit from the experiences of adversity. Reform in attitude and practices, changes in leadership, may be indicated.

Both company and union, as they grow up in their relations with one another, must learn to use, and not abuse, the arbitration process. They must feel that the only good decision in a discipline problem is the correct one. On the one hand, they must appreciate that the loss of a salvageable employee through an error in discipline is bad for the company as well as the workers. On the other hand, they should appreciate that the retention of an employee who should be discharged is bad for the workers as well as the company.

They must acquire more understanding of the arbitrator's functions. In the long catalogue of thankless jobs, the task of deciding whether or not a man should be disciplined ranks high. If the arbitrator seems to the company to be too merciful at times, the critics should place themselves in his position. And it may be, in any event, that the quality of mercy is quite a desirable ingredient of industrial relations. Mercy that is not just weakness is generally respected.

This above all: Management and union alike, in their dealings with one another in this difficult field, and in their attitude toward the arbitrator, must acquire patience and understanding.

APPENDIX

General. For a full-dress presentation of arbitral review of the subject of discharge for cause, see 1 Washington University Law Quarterly (Fall, 1949) pages 71 ff. See also Gollub, Discharge for Cause, New York Department of Labor, Division of Research and Statistics, Special Bulletin No. 221, 1948 (a study of New York State Board of Mediation arbitrations on subject). For an excellent doctoral dissertation (unpublished, available in typewritten form) see Paul Prasow, An Examination of the Role of Arbitration Principles in an Emerging Industrial Jurisprudence (1948), University of So. Cal. (Exceptionally good in problems of absenteeism). As a specialized study, see Luck and Terrican, Trends in Collective Bargaining Contracts in the State of Indiana, Indiana Business Studies, No. 3, Bureau of Business Research, School of Business, Indiana University (July 1950). See also list of collateral readings on disciplinary problems in Shulman and Chamberlain, Cases on Labor Relations, Foundation Press, 1949.

Just Cause. For policy in discipline cases, see Prasow, *op cit supra.* Purpose of discipline, in re Boston & Maine Transportation Co., 5 LA 3 (1946). Question of just cause involves question of extent of discipline, in re E. I. Du Pont De Nemours & Co., Inc., 9 LA 345 (1947). Unequal penalties for same offense, in re Dwight Mfg. Co., 10 LA 786 (1948). Just Cause as varied by plant need, in re American Woolen Co., 5 LA 371 (1946); in re Pierce Governor Co., Inc., 8 LA 541 (1947). Discrimination as morally unjust, in re Birmingham Slag Co., 12 LA 57 (1948). "The arbitrator believes neither in assessing discipline on a mass basis or in excusing wrongful acts on the part of some on the theory that others have committed those acts and escaped disciplinary action. Each case should be carefully weighed with the facts present and decision made on that basis."—a case where different penalties were inflicted for approximately the same offense: in re Vickers, Inc., 6 LA 663 (1947) at 665. Effect of past record, in re Curtiss-Wright Corp., 11 LA 139 (1948). As an example of where an arbitrator quotes from legal authority in discussing just cause, see in re National Bedding and Upholstery Mfgrs. Board of Trade, 10 LA 813 (1948) at page 817. For presentation of concept of good cause in light of NLRB and court decisions, see in re Submarine Signal Co., 4 LA 57 (1945), pages 64 and 65. Past record as bearing upon just cause, in re Chicago Hardware Foundry Co., 1 ALAA §67,502 (1946), Shulman and Chamberlain, page 419. Just cause in *de facto* probationary period, in re Park Sherman Co., 2 LA 199 (1946). As to arbitral review of reasonableness of penalty, see in re New York Car Wheel Co., 7 LA 183 (1947) at 190: "Normally I do not believe that an arbitrator should substitute his judgment for that of the company as to the appropriate penalty in discipline cases." See also in re Allis-Chambers Mfg. Co., 8 LA 149 (1947), where contract was construed so as not to give arbitrator power to examine severity of just discipline. For general considerations, see in re Gardner-Richardson Co., 11 LA 957 (1948), at 960.

Contract Provisions Concerning Discipline. As an example of a contract clause giving an employer power to suspend, but not discharge, prior to hearing before arbitrator (if hearing requested), see in re Bethlehem Steel Co., 6 LA 570 (1947). See also in re Continental Can Co., 6 LA 363 (1947). As an example of contract provision regarding discharge of probationary employees, see in re Ford Motor Co., 6 LA 853 (1946). In general, see Odell, Disciplinary Clauses in Union Contracts, Circular 13, Industrial Relations Section, California Institute of Technology, May 1947; BNA, Collective Bargaining Negotiations and Contracts, Contract Clause Finder, page 40ff; CCH Labor Law Reporter, 4th ed., vol. 5, §52,051ff. For example of contract terms permitting arbitrator to disturb disciplinary action if it is found to be "unreasonable," see in re Ford Motor Co., 7 LA 419 (1947). For example of contract terms providing that employee accused of certain offenses "will not be discharged or dismissed from the premises until and unless the arbitrator so decides," see in re Lou Seidman & Co., 9 LA 653 (1948). For contract provision re production standards, see in re L. F. Fales Machine Co., 7 LA 935 (1947), at 937.

Proof. The burden of proof may be placed by contract upon the grievant. See in re Art Metal Works, Inc., 8 LA 340 (1947), where contract provided: "3. Grievances arising out of any action taken by the Employer in discharging, transferring, suspending any regular employee, provided however that if any such grievance is carried to arbitration, the arbitrator shall not substitute his judgment for that of management and shall only reverse the action or decision of management if he finds that management has acted arbitrarily and in bad faith, or in violation of the express terms of this agreement." For burden of proof in railway cases, see in re Southern Pacific Co., 2 LA 346 (1945). In general see in re Central Boiler & Mfg. Co., 11 LA 354 (1948), at page 357: "It is as true in an arbitration as it is in a court action that one who alleges the affirmative of an issue or raises an affirmative defense has the burden of proving it." Evidence obtained by illegal search excluded, in re Campbell Soup Co., 2 LA 27 (1946). For burden of proof in discharge for union activity, see in re Grayson Heat Control, Ltd., 2 LA 335 (1945), at 338. Burden of proof in cases involving absence without leave, in re American Steel and Wire Co., 12 LA 47 (1948). But note that it is difficult for company to prove absence without cause when confronted with medical certificate, in re Tennessee Coal, Iron & R. R. Co., 11 LA 1127 (1948). Disciplinary action based upon charge of fellow employee whose identity company withholds cannot be sustained, in re Murray Corporation of America, 8 LA 713 (1947). In accident cases, employer's unwitnessed opinion not enough to discipline employee, in re Tennessee Coal, Iron & R. R. Co., 11 LA 1127 (1948). Proof in incompetence case, in re Heil Co., 12 LA 808 (1949); in re Kaiser Company, Inc., 4 LA 346 (1946); in re General Controls Co., 11 LA 722 (1948). Burden of proof as modified by length of service, in re American Smelting & Refining Co., 7 LA 147 (1947). Difficulty of proof in charges of dishonesty, in re Southern Indiana Gas & Electric Co., 6 LA 89 (1946). Use of prior confidential reports, in re Consolidated Vultee Aircraft Corp., 10 LA 907 (1948). For illustration of difficulty of proof of instigating work stoppage, see Copco Steel & Engineering Co., 11 LA 414 (1948). Where employer's proof collapsed because he failed to produce informant-employees at hearing, in re Gaylord Container Corp., 10 LA 439 (1948). Employer's attempt to prove by presumption with no witnesses, in re Malone & Hyde, Inc., 5 LA 443 (1946). Burden of proof in demotion for incompetence, in re Owl Drug Co., 10 LA 498 (1948). Discharge made without adequate investigation, in re Consolidated Vultee Aircraft Corp., 9 LA 510 (1948).

Discharge, Reinstatement, Back Pay. For contract terms making employees "automatically" subject to discharge for certain reasons, see in re Dayton Malleable Iron Co., 8 LA 680 (1947). Discharge upheld, but not until ninety days to permit employee to get another job, in re Faton Realty Corp., 8 LA 304 (1947). Discharge approved because of fighting, but reemployment recommended, in re Branch River Wool Combing Co., 10 LA 237 (1948). Age and maturity of grievant as a factor in discharge, in re International Harvester Co., 11 LA 1007 (1948). Role of poor working conditions, in re Thor Corp., 10 LA 321 (1948). Role of personality clash with supervisor, in re A.B.C. Steel & Wire Co., 7 LA 479 (1947). Discharge attributable to personal grudge of plant guard (prejudice because of color) set aside: in re Bethlehem Steel Co., 2 LA 187 (1945). Bad blood between supervisor and employee as mitigating factor, in re Dayton Malleable Iron Co., 8 LA 688 (1947). See also in re Knautter-Weber Tool Works, 2 LA 408 (1945). Unauthorized work stoppage held to warrant discharge (citing many decisions) in re Lake Shore Tire & Rubber Co., 2 LA 455 (1946). Where contract interpreted to defer discharge until award of arbitrator, discharged employee entitled to back pay until that time, in re Modernage Furniture Corp., 4 LA 221 (1946). Unemployment compensation benefits must be taken into account. In re—Metropolitan Life Insurance Co., Inc., 2 LA 561 (1945), at page 563: "May I also observe that, under the laws of the Commonwealth of Pennsylvania, all money received . . . as unemployment insurance . . . must be refunded to the Commonwealth by him." With regard to duty of discharged employee to seek work elsewhere, see in re Shakespeare Company, 9 LA 813 (1948), and in re Gardner-Richardson Co., 11 LA 957 (1948). Contract may forbid withholding back pay upon reinstatement by arbitral award, in re International Harvester Co., 6 LA 73 (1946).

Layoff. Layoff for disciplinary purposes may violate layoff and seniority clauses, in re Eagle-Picher Mining & Smelting Co., 6 LA 544 (1947). Policy of applying layoff penalty only when production is slack is discriminatory, and also when it makes no distinction between habitual offender and first offender, in re Bethlehem Steel Co., 7 LA 482 (1947).

Warnings. Contract construed to require warning before discharge action in all cases, and to prevent company from dismissing employees for insubordination without warning. In re Cedartown Textiles Inc., 8 LA 360 (1947). The Arbitrator (Griffin) observed at page 362:

"Many contracts specifically provide that certain offenses such as drunkenness, dishonesty, and gross insubordination will not require warnings before discharge. Typical of such contract provisions are these words:

"The Employer shall not discharge any employee without just cause, and shall give at least one warning notice of the complaint against such employees in writing and a copy of same to the Union affected, except that no warnings need to be given to an employee before he is discharged if the cause of such discharge is dishonesty, drunkenness, or recklessness resulting in serious accidents while on duty or the carrying of unauthorized passengers." (Central States Carriers and International Brotherhood of Teamsters–AFL).[1]

Another contract provides:

"No employee shall be suspended or discharged except for major offenses without having first been notified that a repetition of the offense, or other major offenses, will make him liable to discharge. Such notice may be given by the foreman or other representative of the Company." (Pure Oil Co. and Oil Workers International Union–C.I.O.)[2]

"Thus the procedure would have been for the Company to renegotiate its agreement on warnings in order to provide for specific exceptions."

For example of general duty to warn before discharge, see in

[1] Collective Bargaining Negotiations and Contracts 40: 253.

[2] Collective Bargaining Negotiations and Contracts 40: 253.

re International Association of Machinists, 7 LA 231 (1947). Where discipline based on series of offenses, company should not discharge before it takes lesser forms of discipline, e.g. warning, in re Sears Roebuck & Co., 6 LA 211 (1947).

Demotion. See in re Nat'l Bedding and Upholstery Mfgrs. Board of Trade, 10 LA 813 (1948), at page 817: ". . . the mere fact Mr. Baum was not competent to function any longer as an engineer did not justify his discharge. Some agreements expressly provide for the transfer of such employees to less difficult jobs. See Bulletin 689, U. S. Dept. of Labor, 1942, p. 139. Unfortunately, the Arbitrator has not been able to find any case or text discussion of the obligation of the employer when the contract fails to contain such an express provision but does guarantee seniority on a plant-wide basis. In the absence of such authority, the Arbitrator is inclined to believe and states the rule to be that the employer is obligated to offer transfer to a less difficult job if one is available and not occupied by a person with superior seniority."

For contract term giving company right to demote provided not arbitrary or discriminatory, and placing burden of proof on union, see in re Owl Drug Co., 10 LA 498 (1948). Demotion upheld where employee (supervisor) transferred to nonsupervisory job because of failure to follow instructions, poor work attitude. In re Copeland Refrigeration Corp., 8 LA 923 (1947). Contract construed to prevent employer from demoting for disciplinary reasons. In re Reynolds Alloys Co., 2 LA 554 (1943). Employer ordered to offer lower-rated job in case where demotion, rather than discharge, was proper action. In re Jarecki Machine & Tool Co., 3 LA 40 (1946). Demotion held improper under circumstances, in re Gardner-Richardson Co., 11 LA 957 (1948). Downgrading for carelessness held not authorized by contract, in re Kelly-Springfield Tire Co., 9 LA 480 (1947). See also in re International Harvester Co., 14 LA 882 (1950). Incompetence in position to which promoted should have resulted in demotion rather than discharge, in re Acme Limestone Co., 6 LA 921 (1947). See also in re Kansas Motors, 2 LA 283 (1945). Demotion held not good disciplinary action for carelessness, in re Kelly-Springfield Tire Co., 9 LA 480 (1947).

Transfer. "We do not contest the right of the Company unilaterally to transfer employees within an occupation group (See opinion in issue #3). But that right carries with it an obligation of reasonableness. If this right were without limitation, the Company could work the discharge of many employees by transferring them to codes for which the employee had no prior experience or training, and then discharge because of the lack of qualification."

In re Curtiss-Wright Corp., 11 LA 139 (1948), at page 141. For problems involved in transfer from one seniority unit to another as disciplinary measure, see in re Ford Motor Co., (Opinion A-34, 1943), Shulman and Chamberlain, 547.

Withholding of Vacation Pay. See in re Liberty Plating Co., 9 LA 505 (1947). As penalty for work stoppage in violation of agreement, employees directed to make up time lost on straight time rate. In re Full Fashioned Hosiery Manufacturers of America, 2 ALAA §67, 542 (1946). See also in re Terre Haute Malleable & Mfg. Co., 9 LA 526 (1948).

Loss of Seniority. Loss of four years' seniority upheld as disciplinary action. In re John Deere Tractor Co., 5 LA 534 (1946). Discharge penalty reduced to loss of two years' seniority. In re American Car & Foundry Co., 10 LA 325 (1948).

Denial of Promotion. Contract construed to deprive employer of power to deny promotion for disciplinary reasons. In re Pan American Refining Corp., 9 LA 47 (1947).

Company Rules. Duty to make safety rules: See in re Ford Motor Co. (opinion A-117, 1944). Shulman and Chamberlain, 374. "Protection of employees against safety hazards by the publication and enforcement of safety rules is an accepted duty of Management which Management must discharge however distasteful the task may be to it or to the employees." Duty to negotiate regarding plant rules affecting working conditions, see in re The Timken Roller Bearing Co., 70 NLRB 500, Shulman and Chamberlain, 391. Significance of plant rules as representing statement of policy by company, putting employees on notice as to the company's view of importance of certain breaches of discipline, in re Timken Roller Bearing Co., 4 LA 408 (1944). Duty to promulgate rules in advance of discipline, in re Baltic Metal Products Co., 8 LA 782 (1947). Duty to be clear and comprehensive in rules, in re Reynolds Metal Co., 9 LA 585 (1948). Examples of shop rules: No smoking, in re Baltic Metal Products Co., 8 LA 782 (1947); safety rules, in re U. S. Rubber Co., 10 LA 50 (1948); in re West Virginia Pulp & Paper Co., 10 LA 117 (1947); clocking another's time card, in re Reynolds Metal Co., 9 LA 585 (1948); visiting, in re Riley Stoker Corp., 7 LA 764 (1947); tardiness, distribution of union literature, in re Douglas Aircraft Co., Inc. 3 LA 598 (1946); bringing alcohol into plant, in re John Deere Tractor Co., 10 LA 319 (1948); stealing, carelessness, defacement of property, obscenity, in re Trane Co., 12 LA 559 (1949); running in plant, in re McInerney Spring & Wire Co., 11 LA 679 (1948). Limits of employer's rule making power, in re Riley Stoker Corp., 7 LA 764 (1947). Promulgation of rules before effectiveness, in re United States Spring & Bumper Co., 5 LA 109

(1946); in re Western Express Co., 10 LA 172 (1948). Plant rules not automatic discharge cause, in re Campbell Soup Co., 10 LA 200 (1948). Effect of employer's condonations, in re Allis-Chalmers Mfg. Co., 8 LA 177 (1947); in re Douglas Aircraft Co., 3 LA 598 (1946). Mitigating circumstances (inaccessibility of time clock), in re Adler Mfg. Co., 4 LA 700 (1946). Arbitrability of "price list" in collective bargaining agreement, in re Sacramento City Lines Inc., 11 LA 157 (1946). Importance of consistency in plant rule enforcement, in re Bethlehem Steel Co., 6 LA 453 (1947); in re Metal Auto Parts Co., 6 LA 443 (1947).

Inefficiency. Where inefficiency attributable to union work, remedy may be to relieve employee of job as shop steward, in re International Shoe Co., 8 LA 746 (1947). Assignment of work not in good faith, in re Merchants Fire Dispatch, 12 LA 407 (1949). Failure to meet changed production standards as basis for discharge, 7 LA 163 (1947). A case illustrating clerical job of collecting data to justify discharge for failure to meet production standards, in re International Shoe Co., 7 LA 191 (1947). Faulty equipment as real cause of accident and damage to company property, in re Potash Co. of America, 3 LA 403 (1946). Lack of training as a cause, in re Bastian-Morley Co., Inc., 3 LA 412 (1946). Demotion before proper opportunity to demonstrate qualifications, in re United Aircraft Products, Inc., 10 LA 143 (1948). Inexperience versus carelessness, in re A Gross Candle Co., Inc., 9 LA 61 (1947). Extenuating circumstances (family difficulties) in re Curtiss-Wright Corp., 11 LA 139 (1948). Bird-dogging as real reason for discharge, in re Consolidated Vultee Aircraft Corp., 11 LA 7 (1948). Failure to discharge before end of probationary period, in re Sager Lock Works, 12 LA 495 (1949). A striking example of case where arbitrator sustained discharge for inefficiency in spite of sentiment: "Every human sympathy, as well as natural impulse, counsels reinstatement," in re Ben Myers Co., 12 LA 599 (1949). Transfer rather than discharge the remedy, in re Burkhardt Co., 10 LA 807 (1948). Reinstatement ordered on probationary basis in view of poor company procedures, in re Art Chrome Co. of America, 11 LA 932 (1948). Production standards held under contract to be a matter for collective bargaining, in re International Harvester Co., 11 LA 1168 (1949). Discharge for excessive scrap of top rated employee held unjustified under circumstances, in re General Controls Co., 8 LA 661 (1947). Failure to instruct on duties as ground for mitigation in discipline for negligence, in re Taggart Corp., 8 LA 368 (1947). Unsatisfactory work tied in with unsatisfactory machinery, in re McDonnell Aircraft Corp., 3 LA 158 (1946). Inefficiency attributable to overanxiety for advancement, in re Sherron Metallic Corp., 3 LA 154 (1946). The problem of the neurotic employee: "The arbitrator seeks reassurance that a company has done everything possible to enable the employee to adjust to normal work-life," but cannot require a company to "subordinate its function of producing efficiently and safely to the maintenance of a human relations policy," in re Whitin Machine Works, 10 LA 707 (1948), at page 712. Inefficiency attributable to assignment of excessive work, in re Borden's Farm Products, 8 LA 593 (1947). Defects in a system of efficiency ratings, in re International Register Co., 8 LA 285 (1947). Inefficiency as cause for denial of promotion, in re Inland Steel Co., 4 LA 657 (1946). Discharge for inefficiency after unreasonable denial or request for transfer, in re Caterpillar Tractor Co., 6 LA 593 (1947). Inefficiency as related to job security, in re R. H. Macy & Co., Inc., 4 LA 131 (1946). To discharge for all acts of carelessness is self-defeating: in re Nineteen Hundred Corp., 6 LA 709 (1946), at 711. Effect of retention beyond probationary period: if keeping on beyond probationary period indicates acceptance and approval of competency, it will be a factor in arbitrator's mind: in re Master Electric Co., 5 LA 339 (1946); in re Neches Butane Products Co., 5 LA 307 (1946). See in re Master Electric Co., 5 LA 339 (1946), at 340, for agreement between company and union facilitating necessary reclassification to lower rates after war. Where company alleges inefficiency apparently as after-thought, not convincing—in re International Register Co., 8 LA 285 (1947). Efficiency ratings may not be accurate or fair, *id.* Example of arbitrator's unwillingness to insist on retention of employees where retention might be potentially dangerous, in re Shreiber Trucking Co., 5 LA 430 (1946); in re Ward Baking Co., 8 LA 837 (1947); in re Carnegie-Illinois Steel Corp., 5 LA 179 (1946), or where employee has demonstrated a poor work attitude, in re Diamond Alkali Co., 5 LA 105 (1946). Incompetence as result of too rapid upgrading, in re Federal Machine & Welder Co., 5 LA 60 (1946). Discharge for failure to meet production standard requires assembly of data, in re International Shoe Co., 7 LA 191 (1946). Production standard held to be a matter of collective bargaining, not to be imposed unilaterally, in re Celanese Corp. of America, 11 LA 1168 (1949). Importance of time sheets and records to support charges of inefficient production, in re Heil Co., 12 LA 808 (1949). Effect of bad working conditions on production standards, in re Dwight Mfg. Co., 10 LA 786 (1948). Excessive work assignments, in re Borden's Farm Products, 8 LA 593 (1947). Incompetency due to union activity, in re International Shoe Co., 8 LA 747 (1947).

Absenteeism, etc. For example of contract clauses relating to absence, see in re Rock Hill Printing and Finishing Co., 14 LA 153 (1949). For example of faked illness claims, see in re Pan American Petroleum Corp., 2 LA 541 (1946). But suspicion not enough, in re International Harvester Co., 9 LA 484 (1947); in re Tennessee Coal, Iron & R. R. Co., 11 LA 909 (1947). Attempt to discharge for first offense—absence without leave, in re Huron Milling Co., 4 LA 448 (1946). Example of too rigid interpretation of company absence rules, in re Erie Resistor Corp., 5 LA 161 (1946); in re Volco Brass and Copper Co., 7 LA 471 (1947). Company technicality in construing failure to notify rule, in re International Harvester Co., 6 LA 73 (1946). Contract provision that three days' absence for any cause other than personal illness would terminate employment applied by arbitrator to uphold discharge, in re St. Louis Car Co., 5 LA 572 (1946). Absence without leave may arise from employee failure to appreciate that one does not have a right to a vacation at a certain time, in re Bethlehem Steel Co., Inc., 11 LA 629 (1948). Excessive absenteeism as ground for disciplinary action, in re Chrysler Corp., 10 LA 771 (1948). Habitual illness, in re Celanese Corp. of America, 9 LA 143 (1947). Transportation factor as mitigating circumstance, in re Homestead Valve Mfg. Co., 6 LA 627 (1946). Inflexible denial of leave at Christmas period as real cause, in re Pittsburgh Metallurgical Co., Inc., 12 LA 95 (1949). Change in policy without sufficient notice: in re Cone Finishing Co., 12 LA 771 (1949); in re John Deere Tractor Co., 11 LA 548 (1948); in re Bethlehem Steel Co., Inc., 11 LA 629 (1948). Discharge for absence for physical reasons, in re Kendall Refining Co., 11 LA 150 (1948).

Fighting. Assault on foreman. See in re Ford Motor Co. (1944), Shulman and Chamberlain, 415; in re Pioneer Gen-E-Motors Corp., 3 LA 486 (1946); in re Hiram Walker & Sons, Inc., 10 LA 675 (1948); in re Terminal Cab Co., Inc., 7 LA 780 (1947). Inadvisability of single penalty: in re Trane Co., 14 LA 1039 (1950). Cannot deny right of self-defense: in re Consolidated Vultee Aircraft Corp., 11 LA 153 (1948).

Refusal to Take Job. Refusal to take job may suggest need for improved personnel relations, see in re Star Carbonizing Co., 6 LA 76 (1947), at page 78. Where company has contributed to misimpression that employee can accept layoff instead of offered work, company must clarify situation before discharge: in re Vulcan Detinning Co., 6 LA 198 (1947). Where balking at orders is due to misunderstanding of job duties, sometimes a failure in negotiating process is indicated: in re General Magnetic Co., 2 LA 181 (1946). Insubordination consisting of refusal to accept instruction as ground for discharge: in re Micamold Radio Corp., 3 LA 459 (1946). An example of what may be considered excessive leniency in arbitration, in re Finders Mfg. Co., 3 LA 846 (1946). Clearcut refusal to accept work as justification for discharge or other discipline, in re Goodyear Clearwater Mills, 6 LA 117 (1947); in re American Can Co., 11 LA 46 (1948); in re John Deere Tractor Co., 5 LA 561 (1946); in re National Tube Co., 9 LA 549 (1947). Where contract permits employee to refuse transfer, refusal not insubordination, in re Moore Enameling & Mfg. Co., 7 LA 459 (1947). Employer should let employee know he is being ordered, in re Dairymen's League Cooperative Assn., 11 LA 1113 (1948). Order should be clear, in re Boeing Aircraft Co., 8 LA 303 (1947). Refusal to work overtime—unreasonable request, in re Ford Motor Co., 11 LA 1158 (1948). Employee had no right to dispute employer's setting production standards, in re National Machine Co., 5 LA 97 (1946).

Strike. For excellent article, see Daykin, The No Strike Clause, 11 U of Pitts L Rev, 13ff (1949). Mere participation not enough for discharge, in re Bethlehem Steel Co., 2 LA 195 (1945). Shirking job as opposed to participation, in slowdown, in re Ford Motor Co. (1943), Shulman and Chamberlain, page 407. For example of no strike clause, see in re John R. Evans & Co., 6 LA 414 (1946). Obligation not to strike may exist without express no strike clause, in re Simplicity Pattern Co., 7 LA 180 (1947). Significance of no strike clause, in re Bethlehem Steel Co., 2 LA 194 (1945). Underlying causes of violation of no strike clause, in re Eberhard Mfg. Co., 4 LA 419 (1944); in re Armour & Co., 5 LA 697 (1946); in re U. S. Rubber Co., 8 LA 44 (1947). Effect of settlement agreement on sanctions for violation, in re South Side Dye House, Inc., 10 LA 533 (1948); in re Davidson Mfg. Co., 8 LA 698 (1947); in re Cutter Laboratories, 9 LA 187 (1947). Kinds of discipline: demotion, in re Bethlehem Steel Co., 10 LA 186 (1948). Denial of vacation pay: in re Perley A. Thomas Car Works, 8 LA 394 (1947). Blanket denial of merit increases: in re John Waldron Corp., 5 LA 473 (1946). Replacement of strikers during strike period: in re Lancaster Iron Works, Inc., 4 LA 760 (1946). Selective discipline: (1) against union officials: in re John Deere Ottumwa Works, 11 LA 675 (1948); in re Stockham Pipe Fittings Co., 4 LA 744 (1946); in re Mueller Brass Co., 3 LA 285 (1946); in re Nathan Mfg. Co., 7 LA 3 (1947); in re Armour & Co., 8 LA 758 (1947); in re Borg-Warner Corp., 4 LA 4 (1945). (2) Employer must prove leadership or other basis of responsibility: in re American Steel & Wire Co., 5 LA 193 (1946); in re Rheem Mfg. Co., 8 LA 85 (1947). Illegal activity during strike (mass picketing, etc.); in re Swift & Co., 12 LA 108 (1948); in re Pioneer Mill Co., Ltd., 6 LA 644 (1947); in re John Morrell & Co., 12 LA 82 (1949); in re Armour & Co., 11 LA 600 (1948); in re

Cudahy Packing Co., 11 LA 1138 (1948); in re International Harvester Co., 9 LA 944 (1948). Effect of union cooperation in ending strike: in re Cumberland Undergarment Co., Inc., 5 LA 766 (1946).

Slowdown, etc. (1) Also prohibited by no-strike clause: in re Chrysler Corp., 9 LA 789 (1947); (2) attitude of an arbitrator toward: in re Inspiration Consolidated Copper Co., 9 LA 454 (1948); (3) mitigating circumstances: in re Franklin Tanning Co., 9 LA 167 (1947); (4) propriety of: in re General Steel Castings Corp., 11 LA 834 (1948). Discipline for slowdown: instigating slowdown: in re Yale Rubber Mfg. Co., 9 LA 447 (1948); group participation, group discipline: in re Gloucester Fisheries, 5 LA 466 (1946); attempt to discharge employee who urged slowdown: in re Corn Products Refining Co., 3 LA 242 (1946). What is a slowdown? in re Aluminum Cooking Utensil Co., 5 LA 85 (1946). Hindering production: in re John Deere Tractor Co., 10 LA 165 (1948). Work stoppage: proper discipline for: in re Auto-Lite Battery Corp., 3 LA 122 (1946); mitigating circumstances: in re C. G. Hussey & Co., 7 LA 590 (1947).

www.ingramcontent.com/pod-product-compliance
Lightning Source LLC
LaVergne TN
LVHW011817200926
848484LV00005B/1225